A COMEDIC GUIDE TO MONEY

COLIN RYAN

Haver Press
Burlington, VT 05401
www.HaverPress.com

Library of Congress Control Number: 2018939684

Names and identifying characteristics of students, study participants, and others have been changed.

First print edition May 2018.

Jacket Design by Colin Ryan, Lindsey Lathrop and Miladinka Milic. Layout by Carolyn Sheltraw.

For information about special discounts for bulk purchases, please contact the author at info@colinryanspeaks.com. Colin Ryan is a professional keynote speaker and entertainer. For more information or to book an event visit www.colinryanspeaks.com.

ISBN 978-0-9997168-0-9
ISBN 978-0-9997168-1-6 (ebook)

PRAISE FOR
A COMEDIC GUIDE TO MONEY

"This books makes money crystal clear, and it will change your understanding of money. I know because it changed mine. Plus, I'm going to buy my dad a copy!"

– Owen, college student

"As the financial landscape becomes more complex and its management responsibilities become more personal, it is vital for everyone to increase the power of their financial knowledge in order to make the right choices and decisions for them. In this book, Colin provides the knowledge and tools you need in a way you won't soon forget!"

– Daniel Hebert, Director of Professional Development, Jump$tart Coalition
www.jumpstart.org

"It's simple. If you want to live a successful life, then you must master how to build wealth and protect it. In this book, Colin pours his heart out and gives you the tools to do just that! He has deconstructed what others have deemed a complicated subject and provided you with the HOW and WHY of building a better relationship with your money. I promise you will not be let down. My friend, open this book and allow Colin to be your personal guide on how to master your money!"

– Dr. Laymon Hicks, Speaker, Author
and Leadership Strategist
www.LaymonHicks.com

"This book is an easy, casual, not-at-all-grueling guide to how to make the most out of my life financially so I don't have to let money hold me back. It paves a clear path to avoiding debt, and saving enough to make the purchases that *I* want to make. It provided me with clear techniques about how to be financially responsible and save money like a pro, as well as making money a little less-intimidating. I am glad I now have the resources I need to avoid financial trouble before it starts."

– Zoey, high school student

"As a parent of two teenage boys, I was anxious to give my kids financial savvy and help them create a solid foundation for their future. But when do teenagers want to hear a parental lecture about the value of saving money?!? NEVER!!! That's where Colin Ryan comes in. This book is an accessible, practical, useful and FUNNY guide that kids will want to read!"

— Jean Reinsborough, MA, LADC, SEP, Psychologist-Masters

"Among the hundreds of clients I coach each year, one thing shows up every time: their understanding (or lack thereof) when it comes to money. Facing fear and saving money have not only been the backdrop of Colin's life story, but of every one of my clients' stories as well. There has not been a book that better tackles the subject of money and our shame around mismanaging it than 'A Comedic Guide to Money.' Colin Ryan offers us a vehicle to make immediate change in our habits and our relationship to money, so that by doing so we can begin to find the freedom we all crave."

— Amy Magyar, PCC, CVCC, Professional Coach
www.fromwithincoaching.com

"There are too few financial education classes in schools today and young people are left in the dark about their financial future. This book is an easy way into the world of money and provides a lot of the information you'll need to start your financial story. Plus it's funny which alleviates the stress and stigmas that surround money.

Despite always having a relatively fearful relationship with money, this book has given me the confidence to see that dealing with money isn't as daunting as it may seem."

– Sean, high school student

"When I met Colin I knew he was destined for great things. He is authentic, funny, engaging, and knows how to connect with his audience. He is living his passion and dream. If you want a humorous and realistic approach to handling money, this book is a must-read!"

– Colleen Wedge, high school teacher,
Champlain Valley Union High School

"Most people don't think about money being a funny topic. And yet Colin Ryan has taken this extremely important subject and translated it in digestible, relatable and humorous fashion. This is the money book that you will actually finish reading!"

– Jake Ballentine, Motivational Speaker
and Author of Your Number One Goal
www.yournumberonegoal.com

TABLE OF CONTENTS

PROLOGUE:

SIX MONTHS
IN A
SCOTTISH CASTLE

"Aye, fight and you may die. Run, and you'll live. At least a while. And dying in your beds, many years from now, would you be willing to trade all the days from this day to that, for one chance, just one chance, to come back here and stand up and tell our enemies that they may take our lives, but they'll never take our freedom?"

—William Wallace, Braveheart

"The best time to plant a tree was 20 years ago. The second best time is now."

—Chinese proverb

When I was eleven years old, I decided that I wanted to live in the movie *Braveheart*.

I had it all mapped out—I was going to become an eleventh-century Scottish freedom fighter.

Right away, I ran into obstacles.

But it was perfectly reasonable dream for young boy to have. Mainly because it looked a lot like my life at the time. I was led to believe I could run around in the woods, fight bad guys with a sword, and impress girls without showering.

Digging a little deeper, what I really loved about *Braveheart* was that it was a story about passion. It was about a group of people who were less afraid of dying than of not truly living. Every story starts with a conflict, and there is no clearer or more compelling conflict than the fight for your freedom.

After college, I saved up every penny I had, and did the scariest thing I'd ever done. I moved to Scotland. Some college friends and I got six-month international work visas, and we went to live in the capital city of Edinburgh.

Let me just say, if you've seen the movie *Braveheart*, and you think you're prepared to go live in Scotland, that is not enough information. They've made some updates.

I'll never forget the first time I saw a castle, and across from it a Taco Bell. I don't remember that part in the movie.

My first real, grown-up job was at the Royal Bank of Scotland, which was in an actual castle. To be clear, I worked in the mailroom of the castle. Which was in the basement. Historically, basements of castles are dungeons. How appropriate. For six months, I sorted huge bags of mail into smaller bags of mail. A life of passion.

Fortunately, I had a coworker named John. A fifty-two-year-old Scotsman. John made me laugh every single day I worked there. When I introduced myself, the first thing he ever said to me was, "Oh right, you're American." And then he mimed like he was playing a banjo! I couldn't even be mad. That's the most adorable way to stereotype 320 million people.

My other coworkers, Frank and Peter, were also working-class Scottish guys. They may not have been academics, but they were brilliant conversationalists. I learned old Scottish sayings like "*och aye the nu*," dirty jokes, how to properly order a Guinness, and a variety of contradictory theories on what women want.

These conversations took our minds off the work, which was incredibly monotonous. It wasn't a dream job, but for me, it was only temporary. It was a way to pay for train trips around England, Ireland, Wales, and eventually a six-week backpacking adventure across Europe. I could put up with it because it was a means to an end. But for the others, it wasn't just a job for the moment, it was their career. I never dared to ask, but I wondered, "Is this your passion? Is this what you hoped to do with your life?"

I didn't really need to ask, because the answer would've certainly been, "No." Every day, whenever someone irritated or annoyed John, he would stand up and announce loudly how many days he had left until retirement.

"Eight years, nine months, and twenty-seven days."

In his Scottish accent, it sounded charming and depressing at the same time. We were a long way away from "They may take our lives, but they'll never take our freedom!"

John loved to complain about his job, about the leased BMW he hated having to make payments on, and about his bar tab from the previous weekend. Complaining is contagious, so once John started the other guys would join in. They legitimately seemed to love tossing in their few favorites from a long string of bitter catchphrases. "No good deed goes unpunished." "That's how they get you." "The nail that stands out gets hammered down."

My favorite was: "Same old shite, different day." It was the Scottish version of Morgan Freeman's quote from *The Shawshank Redemption*. Where he was playing an actual prisoner.

But John was in a job, not in jail. Then it hit me: John might just be the most inspiring mentor I could ever have, all without him even knowing it. Over the next few months, John taught me many things.

He taught me that I could end up feeling like a prisoner, even outside of jail, if I didn't have a plan to reach my dream. He taught me that complaining about my life would be a sorry substitute for changing my life.

John taught me that our mentors are all around us, either inspiring us to be like them, or to be anything else but them.

But the biggest thing John taught me is that I actually am living in the movie *Braveheart*. Only the enemy of my freedom is not some faraway king. It's in my refusal to take meaningful risks with my life, and in my inability to manage my money.

Facing fear and saving money have been in the background of every scene in the story of my life. Those two habits have allowed me the freedom to fight to find work I'm passionate about, and when I hit a dead end, to summon the courage to take my search elsewhere. John inspired me to understand something I have never forgotten: the key to our freedom is the way we manage our money.

On my last day of work, John leaned over to whisper some great piece of wisdom in my ear. He said something I'll never forget: "Eight years, three months, and twenty-one days."

This has stayed with me always. Every time I've found myself working the wrong job, I've thought of John and then quit. I went through a series of wrong jobs to find work I care about and believe in.

But it was worth it.

Being a speaker who combines comedy with financial advice can be vulnerable, challenging, and incredibly hard work. It asks everything of me. It also just so happens to make me feel fully alive. How do I know this? Because I don't count how many days I have left until I can quit. That, at least to me, is what it means to truly live: do everything you can to find what you love to do, the work that makes you wish you had as many days left as possible.

• • • • • • • •

When I set out to learn the skills of having a better relationship to my money, I quickly found I could reach my other goals in life a lot faster. I wrote this book to give you the same skills that changed my life—how to avoid drowning in debt, how to stop unhealthy spending habits, how to steer clear of scams, and how to save your way out of stress. These skills allow us to enjoy the money we have so it works for us instead of against us.

The best part is you don't need to have a background in finance to learn these skills. I don't have one. I got into this as a blogger, not a banker. I don't look at long columns of data for fun. When I hear the word "amortization," I either cringe or want to take a nap. Sometimes both.

But the simple fact is that we live in a system where what we don't know about money affects us, even limits our ability to have the life we want. Once I admitted to myself this was true, I knew I needed to stand up for my own dream, and learn the skills to having a happy and fulfilling life.

It turns out that money is a pretty fascinating subject, hidden underneath some of the most unappealing-sounding terms you'll ever hear: investing, budgeting, credit cards, interest-bearing accounts, bonds, loans, consumerism, and compound interest. Let's not forget premium flexible annuities. I'm sure you'll agree, these phrases don't tend to bring people running to find out more. But once you understand how these and other financial concepts work, the world of money opens up to you.

Money isn't boring when it's yours.

I'll be honest, I'd much rather have a *painless* money conversation with you. In this book I'll deconstruct the messages we get from pop culture, examine our pre-existing values and assumptions, and break down a seemingly vast world of concepts and terminology into a simple, actionable roadmap toward a better relationship with your money.

CHAPTER 1

LET'S TALK
ABOUT MONEY

Money travels everywhere, crosses all boundaries, languages, and cultures. Money, like water, ripples at some level through every life and place. It can carry our love or our fear. It can flood some of us such that we drown in a toxic sense of power over others. It can nourish and water the principles of freedom, community and sharing. Money can affirm life or it can be used to demean, diminish, or destroy it. It is neither evil nor good; it is an instrument. We invented it, and it belongs squarely in the human experience, but it can be used by and merged with the longings and passions of our soul.

—Lynne Twist, *The Soul of Money*[1]

Let's start things off with a bang by defining the word 'economy.'

"Yes! I was hoping you'd go there!" you're no doubt shouting in excitement right now.

It's a less-than-thrilling finance word, to be sure. But 'economy' simply refers to a system of money. A system in which money flows in and flows out.

That's it.

Countries are economies. So are cities, universities and colleges, and families. If you think about it, each one of us is an economy. Money flows in and out of our lives. It flows in through things like jobs, allowance, and loans from our parents (that we might never pay back). True story: I once found a fifty-dollar bill in a library book. Seriously. It's the reason I think you should read.

Of course money is also flowing out of our lives, as we pay for food, clothes, gas, movies, and all kinds of things.

So, not actually that boring after all.

How well we manage that flow of money is an easy way of measuring how well we're managing our own personal economy. Even massive economies can crash, and when they do, we talk about it. But personal economies crash, too. People go into debt, declare bankruptcy, lose their house or their car. We don't talk about that as much, but we should. We should do anything we can to keep our own personal economy from crashing.

The good news is that not only can we keep it from crashing; we can make it serve our dream.

What do you want to be free to do in your life? Travel the world? Set your own schedule? Do work you believe in? Just think about it. You can reach that dream if you can manage your money.

GAME TIME

Let's play a little game. (It's not really a game, actually. It's not even that exciting—I'm basically throwing a fresh coat of paint on a word association activity.) I'm going to say a word, and then I want you to think of the first word that pops into your head.

Ready?

"Money."

What's the first word that popped into your head?

Over the years, I've gotten really interesting answers. Some people say "Dollar" or "Cash." Because they are very literal. Others say "Power" or "Happiness." Because money tends to separate people into two categories: the haves and the have-nots. Others say "Burritos." Because they're hungry.

One interesting response was when someone said, "Evil." I get it. Money has done incredible damage to huge numbers of people. Or more accurately, the way money has been handled has done damage.

If a word hasn't popped into your mind yet, here are some other questions you could consider:

What is your family like when it comes to talking about money? What is something about money you learned the hard way?

I'm guessing that your word or your answer to one of these questions will help you start identifying your specific relationship with money. We all have one. Anything we handle daily and think about as often as we do money is something we have a relationship with. Think about how many times a day you think about money. *Can I afford to go to that place? What will food cost? My friends' clothes cost more than mine. Will I have enough money for that?* That's a daily relationship.

A relationship with an origin point. We can trace this relationship, which forms your reactions and your prejudices and your fears and your desires about money, back to the first moment when you can recall having an emotional response to money.

I'll give you my word: "Pain."

When I was about eleven years old, I started to experience a feeling typical of middle school kids—all of a sudden I cared what my peers thought about me. What I had worn for years without a problem was suddenly totally humiliating to me, and I couldn't bear to go another minute without changing it.

In my case, it was glasses. I'd had them since third grade. Big plastic rims. So ugly they were almost creepy, way before anyone wore them ironically. The reason I'd had them was because they were from the "covered by our insurance" section of the store. Way in the back, where sometimes they don't even bother turning the lights on.

Of course I wanted a pair of cooler glasses. Florida grandma's wraparound sun blockers. I asked if I could get a pair from the front of the store. The look on both my parents' faces told me I wouldn't get the answer I was hoping for.

A few weeks earlier, my stepdad had found out he was losing his job. I didn't know what that meant, but they explained to me that we were all going to have to make sacrifices.

"We don't have any money coming in," they said. "So we can't afford luxuries right now. You want that pair of glasses, but you don't need them."

I lost that fight, and I walked into school the next day with yet another pair of awkward plastic frames. Original creepster.

That was the first conversation where money became real to me, and from it I learned a few things I have never forgotten: the lack of money can feel shaming, smart spending is about knowing the difference between wants versus needs, and often our small, daily purchases can have ripples that affect our financial picture as a whole.

The reason my word was "pain" is because I realized that money is finite, and that if I spent too much of it, or I succumbed to the voice of temptation that urges me to buy things I don't really need, someday I might experience what it felt like to run out of money. Really run out.

So from eleven years old, I practiced differentiating between wants and needs. I associated spending money with running out of all our money, and maybe even losing our house. I feared debt because debt felt like a kind of death. A death of freedom, perhaps.

It made me an Olympic-level saver.

But for a long time afterwards I had to consciously remind myself that I could afford to spend money on things. That scare echoed for a long time. By not letting it control my life, I came to understand that the point of money is to use it as a tool to have a wonderful life: a life where you do things that make you truly happy, and make the world better for others as well.

In reality, money isn't good or evil. It's simply a tool. How we handle money often tells us more about ourselves than it does about money itself. Like most tools, money can be dangerous, because one thing it can't buy us is a conscience.

YOUR MONEY PERSONALITY

It was author Olivia Mellan who first introduced me to the idea that there are several highly-common money personality types.[2] She describes them in her book *Money Harmony*, and it's really eye-opening to consider which one you are.

SAVER

Savers will save and save, and no matter how high that number gets, she or he will always fear that a mistake or a sudden emergency will clean out that money and lead them to poverty. Savers see money not so much as a way of buying nice things, but as a method of developing security. (They are also called Hoarders, but since I am one I renamed it to something less judgy-sounding).

Common behaviors of Savers:

You bring your own candy into movies. You enjoy checking your account balances and keeping a budget because of how much you enjoy seeing it add up. You don't spend all your allowance, but save some to add the next time you get it. You love a good deal, and you see the one-dollar shirt you found on the clearance rack as a success story you like sharing with friends. (Not everyone gets you.)

SPENDER

While the Saver sees spending money as a painful necessity, Spenders feel great joy in making purchases. More than that, they feel loved, valuable, and even important when they do. Their inner voice tells them, "I deserve this," regardless of whether they can afford it. Spenders know the phrase "retail therapy" all too well, and often medicate negative thoughts or depression by buying new things that don't feel new after a while. They're also super-fun to be around.

Common behaviors of Spenders:

Money doesn't last long in your wallet. You have some money in it one day, but the next day you take it out and it's gone, and you're honestly not sure what you spent it on. If you're old enough, you have at least one credit card, and you'll open more in the future. You have lots of nice things in the closet, in your room, maybe even in every room. You drive a non-piece-of-junk car. You buy things you are excited to show off.

AVOIDER

Avoiders do exactly that—they avoid the subject of money. They're not that interested. They'd rather think about something else. Ask them how much money they have, and they may not know. Ask them what they want to do in the future, and they'll say, "I don't know what I'm doing this weekend, let alone five years from now." If they're being honest, Avoiders know that remaining uninformed about their finances is causing them to miss opportunities to have more money and be more secure. But they don't really think much about it. They are Avoiders, after all.

Common behaviors of Avoiders:

You procrastinate on doing the research before making financial decisions. The less you know about it, the better. You get uncomfortable when the subject of money comes up, either in conversation or in your thoughts. You let your debts stack up because *Yuck, who wants to deal with those*? If you were hoping to save, and your friends invite you out to the mall or a movie, you feel guilty about not sticking to your guns. You may feel guilty later, but you do it anyway.

DONOR

Mellan also calls this category the "Money Monk," because for a Donor, handling money can often be scary or uncomfortable, so she or he doesn't inherently see money as a good thing. Often raised with strong beliefs, either religious and/or political, Donors' parents may have taught them that money is the root of all evil, or that all rich people are greedy and self-serving.

Common behaviors of Donors:

You almost never ask for money or a promotion or for help. You may think it's because you're not confident, but it might actually be that you're afraid desiring money will make you greedy. You usually try to avoid thinking about or dealing with your finances and especially thinking about your future. When you have extra money, you donate it to charities or help cash-strapped friends. It makes you indescribably happy to buy things for other people.

Now one of two things happened. You totally identified with your money personality, or you saw a little bit of yourself in each of the money personalities (this is very common). Congrats, you have a split personality. Just kidding.

TURN THIS CIRCLE INTO A PIE CHART TO REPRESENT WHAT PERCENTAGE YOU ARE OF EACH OF THE MONEY PERSONALITIES YOU CONNECTED WITH.

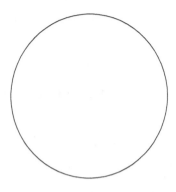

Now that you know which of the four you reso-nate with, here's some good advice to turn them into strengths for you.

ADVICE FOR SAVERS

What makes someone a Saver? Oh, you know, maybe having a parent who loses a job and thus the person is raised in an environment where debt is seen as looming and scary. In other words, my childhood.

Strengths of a Saver: Great self-control—under-stands that money handled carefully leads to security. Always willing to work hard and learn how to do things him/herself rather than pay someone else to do it.

Weaknesses of a Saver: Often struggles with "mental poverty," or the idea that at any second, she or he can be broke. This struggle persists even when the Saver is quite well off. Savers are often ONLY willing to work hard and learn how to do things themselves, instead of paying someone to do it. Savers also struggle with the fear that, in a society where spending money is often associated with being exciting, they are boring.

Advice for Savers: As a saver, it's important to set yourself up with a spending plan. Let's say you have a budget that is designed to show how much you can spend in each category per month. (We'll get into this later.) But for you, dear Saver, these should not only serve as limits, but as targets. If you have set aside fifty dollars a month for food, and you only spend twenty-five dollars this month, allow yourself to spend an extra twenty-five dollars next month.

Often you will feel like you can't make big purchases (e.g., go on trips), but what you really need is to figure out the amount you can afford to spend. Once you turn what feels unknown and scary into a quantifiable number, it'll stop being both.

ADVICE FOR SPENDERS

What makes someone a Spender? Growing up in wealth could do it, where a high-spend lifestyle was modeled. Growing up in an environment where debt is seen as no big deal could do it, too. Or perhaps it's an inability to delay gratification. It's hard to resist the constant pull of consumer society that tells you this new item will make you feel better in a lasting way, even though it won't. Spending becomes a way to get little hits of happiness in place of a deeper, more sustained sense of contentment.

Strengths of a Spender: They are really fun and know how to live the materialistic side of life to its fullest. Spenders have great stories because they are not prevented by price from being out with others and trying things on the expensive end of life's menu.

Weaknesses of a Spender: Many Spenders fall into the trap of conspicuous consumption, meaning they buy things in order to show them off to others. This means they equate possessions with self-worth. If they are honest, most Spenders feel they have very little control over their relationship with money.

Advice for Spenders: Either you control your spending, or it controls you. Be honest with yourself about the realities of overspending. Keep a budget. Pick one category in your life where you spend more money than you should, and stick to a limit there. See what that brings up for you. Hide your credit cards and ask others for help to keep you accountable to not spending beyond your goals. (Also, set goals.) If you're in debt, it's time to spend less and pay off more.

ADVICE FOR AVOIDERS

How does someone become an Avoider? Growing up in a low socioeconomic environment can lead to feelings of fatalism. "What's the point of saving up for tomorrow? I'm just trying to get through today."

Strengths of an Avoider: Avoiders are authentic—they focus on parts of themselves other than money, and that's really good. Avoiders can be fun.

Weaknesses of an Avoider: They can be apathetic, and they can also be reckless. They relentlessly live in the now. Their inability to make plans for the future, or even examine why it's so unpleasant to think about it, leaves them flying blind.

Advice for Avoiders: The thing about money is that it's really just a small set of terms and behaviors, and its more about creating daily habits than spending lots of time thinking about it. If you could do anything with your future, what would it be? Write down three goals and put the list somewhere you'll see it every day. Pick a few areas where you're going to save money, and do those things to move toward your goals, and as a way to practice thinking about your money, read one book about money. (Look at that, you're already doing that one.) Or take a class or workshop on personal finance. You might like it more than you'd guess.

ADVICE FOR DONORS

How does someone become a Donor? A religious upbringing could do it, or any worldview that devalues the material in favor of the spiritual. You could end up distrustful of getting involved with money at all. Or perhaps you grew up in a home where self-sacrifice and generosity were modeled, in which case you're probably a great person, which kind of makes the rest of us feel bad somehow.

Strengths of Donors: You're a good person, and you understand something very important about money—it has great corruptive potential. So you're appropriately cautious, and you often channel that into generosity.

Weaknesses of Donors: You can be suspicious that developing a relationship with money will change you into someone you don't want to be, and make you greedy and materialistic. You're often very hard on yourself, and you have trouble celebrating your successes for fear of becoming self-indulgent.

Advice for Donors: Remind yourself that money isn't all bad—it provides your basic human needs, and it's an awesome way to help your friends out and support good causes. Since you may not really enjoy interacting with your money that much, automating your finances will help: get your paycheck direct deposited into your account, and set up automatic payments (via electronic bill pay or online transfer) for monthly bills, savings goals, and investments/retirement. Set a limit on how much you can give away each month, and then you can have fun doing so without feeling guilty for sabotaging yourself in the process.

Cool? Cool. Oh, and feel free to take Mellan's Money Harmony quiz at www.moneyharmony.com/moneyharmony-quiz.

LEARNING THE LINGO

If now you feel like you have some obstacles ahead of you, don't worry about it. You have to start somewhere. It can be overwhelming but you've already learned so much! So now that we know *how we think* about money, let's look at *how we talk* about it.

We don't.

Many parents demonstrate intense emotions around money. Money is not to be talked about. Money is a secret. Not to be discussed.

But the real secret about money is that everyone wants to talk about it.

A student from a young women's leadership program I was speaking to told me her dad was so secretive about money that when she had to fill out the Free Application for Federal Student Aid (FAFSA), he made her fill her part out completely and then give it to him to so he could add his income and mail it. Very secretive.

Maybe you feel like you can ask your parents what they make and it's no problem. If so, that's great. It's also not very common. Most people are uncomfortable sharing their salary with anyone, let alone their children. Maybe that's because they're afraid you'll tell your friends, and they'll tell their parents. More likely it's because of a false equation that this practice of not talking about money has taught us: My Net Worth = My Self-Worth. The thought has a way of becoming "the money I've been able to make in life is a way of measuring how much value I have as a person."

Can we just acknowledge the obvious truth about this? Which is that it's so wrong? Of course, it's easy to fall into, but on paper we can agree that it's such an unfair way to look at our life or our value.

My Net Worth ≠ My Self-Worth. ≠ for a second.

We often measure ourselves so much against what we want to make, we forget to define what we really need.

As someone who runs a business, when business is good, I feel good. When business is slow, I feel less valuable. The problem with both of those emotions is that they are introduced externally, rather than by me. It took me a long time to pick up on this, and a very short amount of time to recognize that it's a dangerous way to live. You can't survive on other people's feedback of you.

Here's a healthier way to talk about my work: I spend my days helping people live better stories with their lives, and I love what I do. You can't put a price tag on that. The work is worth it because the paychecks are not only the kind I can deposit. It's often emotionally-rewarding as well.

Mixing our net worth with our self-worth makes it's really tricky to talk about money.

Our inability to talk about money has led to a lot of secrecy and shame. When we don't know a term or a concept, we're afraid to admit it and look ignorant. But once you learn the language—terms like Annual Percentage Rate, 401k, 501c3, and, the Rule of 72—money stops being confusing.

Of course, knowing the terms isn't the same as putting them into practice. But money isn't as complex as it may seem. It's more like having braces. Do you (or did you) have braces? I had them for five years. For five years I would regularly go to an orthodontist and get them tightened. And the next day my teeth would hurt. Slowly, over time, I ended up with a set of straight, healthy teeth. It just required a series of small, somewhat painful adjustments over a long period of time to get to there.

Reaching a financial goal is lot like this. In order to win, all you have to do is keep making small, smart, and somewhat uncomfortable decisions over time until you get there.

Money management is almost entirely about behavior modification, or putting good habits into place. Take this one, for example: did you know that making your lunch two or three times a week at home instead of buying it out will save you over $1,000 a year? One small change, repeated, leads to big results.

With money, it's always tempting to take the path of least resistance. But with a little work, there are powerful skills you can pick up that will be far more worth it in the long run.

They're even more important to master when you realize you're living in a culture of consumption.

Time to show you the Matrix, Neo.

CHAPTER 2:

CULTURE OF CONSUMPTION

Advertising constantly promotes the core belief of American culture: that we can re-create ourselves, transform ourselves, transcend our circumstances— but with a twist. For generations Americans believed this could be achieved if we worked hard enough. Today the promise is that we can change our lives instantly, effortlessly . . . by winning the lottery, selecting the right mutual fund, having a fashion makeover, losing weight, having tighter abs, buying the right car or soft drink . . . The American belief that we can transform ourselves makes advertising images much more powerful than they otherwise would be.

— Jean Kilbourne, Can't Buy My Love: How Advertising Changes the Way We Think and Feel[3]

Contentment is natural wealth, luxury is artificial poverty.

— Socrates

It sounds strange to say it now, but as a kid obsessed with movies, Nicolas Cage was my hero. There was just no convincing me that *The Rock* was not perfect in every way. If I'd had the authority, I would have awarded *Con Air* an Oscar for "Best Movie Ever Made." (And the thanks for that new Oscar category goes to: Ricky Bobby!)

It's safe to say people's admiration for Nicolas Cage has changed a lot since I was a kid. It got tougher to be on Team Cage as his ratio of good to bad movies started to equal out, and then tip in the other direction. At some point in the 2000s, Nic began to build what I call "Yikes: The Anthology."

Ghost Rider, Ghost Rider 2: Spirit of Vengeance, Drive Angry, Frozen Ground, Trespass, Rage, Seeking Justice, Stolen, Outcast, Left Behind, Dying of the Light, The Runner, Pay the Ghost, The Trust, Dog Eat Dog, and the list goes on.

Box office bomb after box office bomb. Within just a few years, the Oscar-winning star of *Leaving Las Vegas* had become a solidly direct-to-video actor. It turns out there's something interesting going on here. Maybe you know this, maybe you don't, but Nicolas Cage has been in and out of financial trouble for a while.

It turns out that, just like 40% of American workers, Nicolas Cage lived paycheck-to-paycheck[4], even though according to *Forbes Magazine* he earned $40 million between June 2008 and June 2009.[5] Not only that, but between 1996 and 2011, Nic had earned more than $150 million from acting alone.[6]

How is it even possible that he was broke?

For starters, Cage's uncle is Francis Ford Coppola, director of the *Godfather* trilogy. Many of his relatives were or are in the film business and had considerable wealth. It's likely that Nic experienced a high-earn and high-spend lifestyle from a young age, and began one of his own when he got older. Over the course of his career, the world took notice of his extravagant purchases, which include more than fifty cars, a dozen mansions, two islands, several castles, and a dinosaur skull that cost $276,000.

To be fair, the dinosaur skull is awesome.

But what could explain such financial insanity? In a *Daily Beast* article, a source that worked with him explained, "There's a cluelessness . . . [Cage] has been wealthy since he was 17 years old, and so he's very removed from normal decision-making . . . He never thought about a budget. The mentality was 'that's what houses, cars, diamonds, jets cost,' and he was 'get it, get it, get it.'"[7]

In 2009, around the time the recession was hitting home for a lot of people, Cage sold a castle in Bavaria.[8] Reportedly, his Bavarian neighbors mentioned he had only visited the castle once in the previous year, arriving by helicopter. This made his explanation of the sale less relatable than he was probably aiming for.

"Due to the recession, unfortunately, I was no longer able to keep it," Cage said, while his publicist likely cringed and face-palmed. But selling the castle might be one of Nic's lesser sacrifices. The experience of ongoing financial struggle has led to a very significant change in the actor's public career. Of course I don't know what Nic's goals are as an actor, but from the outside his filmography seems to have morphed from starring in films that will stand the test of time to starring in films he can get paid for.

To be clear, all this kind of makes me like Nicolas Cage even more. Why? Because his artistic shift led me, for the first time, to really examine the financial struggles of an incredibly wealthy and successful individual and ask myself: in his shoes, would I have been any different?

He may have more zeroes on the end of his paychecks, but he's also someone who must often be stressed, worried, and overwhelmed by the challenges of managing money. Like all of us, he lives with the effects of his financial decisions. Thinking about all this, I realized that there are only two categories of people when it comes to spending money: either you control your spending, or your spending controls you.

Where wealth is concerned, we often imagine only half the story about the people we see driving by on occasion. When I think of someone who's rich, I think of the businessperson in the expensive suit, driving a brand new Mercedes, parked in the driveway of an impressively lavish house.

For all we know, inside that house is a stack of bills they don't know how they're going to pay. It could easily be true, but we often forget to tell ourselves that part of the story.

Still an awesome dinosaur skull, though.

SPEND LIKE THE RICH

When you think about rich people, what cars do you picture them driving? Lamborghinis, Bentleys, Murcielagos, Evos, Teslas? What do all these cars have in common? They are all brand new. They all have wheels. And they are all expensive.

Outside of car dealerships, we most frequently see shiny, brand-new cars in TV shows and movies. Entertainment media love new cars, because new cars look cool, and they make their characters look cool.

Take *Iron Man*: Tony Stark pulls up in an Audi R8 (someone had to tell me what kind of car he was driving, because I couldn't actually afford to know things like that).

Or in *Batman Begins*, when he's not driving the Batmobile, Bruce Wayne rolls up in a Lamborghini, the kind with doors that open upward. These are very practical. Not great for drive-through ATMs.

Then of course, there are the *Transformers* movies. I found this ad once that prominently featured the Transformers logo, and alongside it, the GM logo. The ad was basically a shopper's code: if you liked Autobot Ironhide, that's a GMC Topkick, now available at your local dealership. Is Autobot Bumblebee more your style? He nearly died in the first movie, and it was very sad. Now he can live forever, in your driveway, because he's a Chevy Camaro. This is a two-hour car commercial. With people talking, robots, and Megan Fox.

There's a scene in the first *Transformers* movie that perfectly illustrates this car commercial concept. Lead actors Shia Labeouf and Megan Fox are driving around in a junky version of Autobot Bumblebee. Then the vehicle makes them get out and it drives away. As it passes a brand new Chevy Camaro it transforms to look exactly like the other car. It pulls up again, slowly, at car-magazine-camera angles, to the pounding instrumental theme from *Kill Bill*. The car looks sleek, cool, and even sexy. Megan and Shia get back in the car, and she gives him a long look. *That* look.

If we were to pause it there for a second, what would you say is the message of this scene? That's right. If you have a nice car, someone hot will want you.

We laugh at that, because that's an idea we can relate to. If you have shiny, nice things, people will be interested in you. We laugh without pausing to think, *that's a strange message hidden in this blockbuster movie franchise.*

It's also not driving like the rich.

In his book, *The Millionaire Next Door*, Thomas J. Stanley interviews and studies the behavior of actual millionaires. Turns out it's a lot different than we're led to assume.

For example, less than 25% of millionaires buy new cars.

Wait, what?

It gets stranger.

Most millionaires do not buy luxury cars. They buy simply designed, cheaper-to-repair automobiles.

Most have not bought a car in the last two to four years. A typical millionaire habit—and there are many examples of this—is to buy a good, used car, drive it for five or six years (until there are probably things falling off of it), and then buy another good, used car.

Now we're not conditioned to think, "That's probably a millionaire driving by right now, dragging his muffler." But we do think, "Must be nice," when we see somebody driving by in a flashy new vehicle. Only maybe they leased it, and it's looking good. A year or two later, maybe they'll lease another brand new vehicle.

A car lease is a way of renting a car. You pay a few hundred bucks every month for a year or two, and then you give the car back. You don't get any of your money back. You don't have anything to sell or trade in.

I think a car lease is a strategy designed to get us used to driving cars we cannot really afford. Less than one in five millionaires lease cars. Often they save up the money and buy lower-cost cars outright, because they see the lease as a trap—money goes into it; none of it comes back.

The Millionaire Next Door really changed my perspective on people with wealth. Without this kind of research, we can end up viewing consumer culture as one big race to appear wealthier than we are. But all that's really happening is we're acting like the "we wish were rich" crowd instead of the "we're actually rich" crowd.

If we want to learn from others about good money habits, the first step is to separate bad financial examples from good ones. Sort our mentors from our reverse-mentors.

Most millionaires are practical. They live in nice houses, but not necessarily mansions. They drive nice cars, but not necessarily Audi R8s. Also, they are loaded.

They can do what they want with their lives, but they don't toss money around like confetti. They understand that becoming a millionaire doesn't mean that much if you can't figure out how to stay one.

Ironically, despite being one of the most common traits of successful people, being 'cheap' has a negative connotation. Fortunately, the evidence shows what the long-term wealthy think: the bigger the purchase, the bigger the chance to save. Any purchase can be a vote for what you believe in most, whether it's supporting better companies or simply supporting better money habits.

So, think and act like the rich. Drive like the rich. Whenever you can, spend like the rich.

MILLIONAIRE THINKING

Before I attempted to learn how to manage my money, I took an 'ignorance is bliss' approach. I didn't feel like I could turn off the desire to buy things, and I feared that paying more attention to my habits would just overwhelm me more. At least 'ignorance is bliss' sent a few moments of bliss my way. They just never lasted.

Until I took one simple step designed specifically to help me reframe my relationship to my money: I built my first budget.

It was a surprisingly easy and eye-opening step toward understanding where my money went. It helped me to see where I spent too much and where I didn't spend enough. A budget is amazingly useful, because it helps you isolate aspects of your life where your spending is out of control. Despite this, 60% of American adults do not do any kind of monthly budgeting.[9]

Thanks to credit cards, predatory loans, and a steady flow of confusing messages from consumerism, all of us have the temptation and the unfortunate ability to live above our means. But whether we're millionaires, on fixed incomes, or somewhere in between, bad financial habits have a way of catching up with us.

In Stanley's book on the attitudes and habits of American millionaires, he studied all the ways they spend their money.[10] It turns out millionaires are not the people you think they are.

Who are they? You'll have to read the book.

Just kidding. I read it so you don't have to. (You're welcome.) According to Stanley, the most common example of a millionaire in America is a hard-working owner of a successful business who has a nice but not overly fancy house, drives a basic and reliable car, and doesn't live a particularly glamorous lifestyle. They probably have epic vacations though.

The primary values of a typical millionaire are caution, efficiency, and longevity. Spend less than you earn. Take smart risks. Have a safety net.

So to adopt a habit of millionaires, do this:

(What You Spend < What You Earn) x Many Years

Keeping your spending below your earning, year after year after year, will lead you to very good things.

In a 2014 study of over 27,000 American workers, 67% of respondents said they'd find it difficult to meet their financial obligations if their paycheck were delayed for just one week.[11] In fact, 55% of Americans spend more each year than they earn.[12]

To avoid being a statistic, write a new story. Start yourself along the path to becoming a millionaire. It's not impossible. Just know the path is full of challenges, and knowing what they are will help you get around them. So let's point some of them out.

VIVA LAS VEGAS

Have you ever been to Las Vegas? You know, where dreams come true? When I road-tripped there with friends, that's not what I saw. It's a fun, glamorous place. But when I looked closer, I found myself feeling grateful I was too broke at the time to gamble away my money. I saw old ladies flushing coins into slot machines dollar by dollar. I saw people lose big at the craps table. I generally spent my time marveling at how good Vegas casinos are at making your money their money.

It's a business elevated to an art form. They use technology, behavioral psychology, and myriad distractions to make sure that, at the end of the day/month/year, they've made more money on any gambler than any gambler has made on them. "The house always wins" isn't just an expression; it's a mission statement.

Speaking of expressions, you've probably heard this one: "What happens in Vegas stays in Vegas." Man, if only. It turns out that plenty of the casinos' moneymaking strategies are now being used. Here are four.

Strategy #1 – Disorientation: First, casino owners pump their facilities with fresh oxygen to keep their customers alert, active, and spending money. There are no clocks in the casinos, which helps you lose track of time. The air conditioning keeps things chilly enough to keep the gamblers awake. All this causes you to stay longer than you may have intended because you feel great while you're there. When I was in Vegas, it was easy to walk out of a casino and be surprised to discover it was four o'clock in the morning when you thought it was the evening before.

The carpeting is deliberately designed to be visually chaotic and confusing. This draws your eyes up to the level of the machines and not the floor. Casinos also bring you in with flyers for discounts and promotions, intending to make that money back on their slot machines.

You'll also find these strategies in place in most grocery stores.

There are no clocks or windows, and it's often cold to keep you alert. The most harmless display you see is in all likelihood designed by behavioral psychologists and expert researchers to increase purchasing. Stores are arranged to bring in customers with loss leaders (products priced so low the store loses money on them) near the front that increase the likelihood you'll buy the overpriced products elsewhere in the store as well.

Strategy #2 – Monitoring: Casinos monitor their clientele with eye-in-the-sky recordings.[13] Thousands of cameras built into the ceiling can cover more than 80% of a casino. Computer-vision systems automatically scan for specific activity on the floor, such as unattended bags or potentially cheating players.

At big box stores, similar technology is used to monitor traffic patterns inside the store. We think those cameras are for shoplifters, but they're also collecting data on shoppers. For example, a twenty-five-year-old male enters the store and goes to look at flat screen televisions, then buys a DVD boxed set, and while waiting in line for the register, he buys a box of Milk Duds. That's now data to be studied—the customer's traffic patterns, what stimuli may have led to the craving for candy, the effectiveness of displays, and so on.

Strategy #3 – Atmosphere: In Vegas, you buy chances to win money instead of products, so the air is electric with the possibility of winning. All this lowers your inhibition around your money and helps you spend it faster than usual.

Similarly, stores stocked with good-looking staff in new clothes make you feel cool by association, or uncool by comparison. Either feeling encourages you to buy clothes in that store—American Eagle, Urban Outfitters, PacSun, Hollister, Anthropologie, and so on. While you try on those clothes, the music playing makes you feel like you're already out with your friends, mentally reenacting the kind of cool party scenes that were put into our heads by movies and alcohol advertising. To top it off, behavioral economists have found that when you try something on, your mind actually takes possession of the item. At that point, not buying the article of clothing feels like a loss.[14]

Some boutique fashion stores will even offer you a glass of wine. It's that complementary drink technique that casinos are known to offer, loosening your inhibitions and your hold on your wallet. At the end of the day, stores want to make sure you got your invitation to the spending party.

Strategy #4 – Convenience: Casinos bring the mall to you. They install restaurants and shops around their buildings, strategically placed so you have to walk among the slot machines and game tables every time. Plus, with convenient shopping and dining available, they can comp you to go to their in-house buffet. The more time you spend there, the less chance you'll go out to gamble with their competitors. It's kind of like a stealth mall—a business with other businesses inside.

Wal-Mart has a Dunkin Donuts in it. Costco has a fast-order restaurant at the front of the store (which I seem to be incapable of walking past without buying a churro). Luxury hotels often have their own jewelry stores, cafés, bars, grocery stores, and clothing boutiques. They make it so you never have to leave, and all your purchases go on your room tab. Your tab is an opportunity to spend money without paying right away, so you don't think about the cost until you settle your bill at the end of your trip. At that point, it's too late to make a course correction. It's time to go back home and get back to work earning money so you can afford to do this again next year.

THE TREADMILL OF COOL

By now it's becoming clear to you, as it has to me, that our whole culture is designed to create consumers. The system benefits when you spend. That's how the system runs. Capitalism is a culture of consumers.

It's a constant challenge not to overspend when we live in a culture constantly pressuring us to do just that. It's up to us to figure out how to consume without being consumed. We are repeatedly promised that joy, happiness, and fulfillment come from buying things. There's a lot to learn not only by studying the influences of those messages, but also by analyzing society's financial reverse-mentors, too.

Think about this. For most of us, the idea of giving up our smartphone is unwelcome. And not just because we want to stay connected. We'd also stand out from our peers, and not in a good way. Over a few years, the telecommunications industry turned a household utility into a status symbol, and then a symbol of belonging. Without a smartphone, you don't belong. If you still have an old one, you seem like you can't afford what the people around you can. With a new one, your life appears to be better somehow.

Suddenly a smartphone is another way of determining whether or not you belong to the right group.

It's unfair to consumers, but from a marketing perspective, it's brilliant. They made a boring device cool. Once you get customers to see something as cool (usually by getting enough people to adopt it), its cost goes up. Both on individual sales and over time as well, because cool is always changing.

It's called perceived obsolescence.

Perceived obsolescence is when the value or usefulness of a product doesn't necessarily change, but it's perceived value changes. Products lose value not when they stop working, but rather when they say something negative about you—that you don't have the money (and ultimately, the status) to have this year's version of the product. This is how something stops being cool long before it stops being useful.

Technology has always been about rapid change, but once it got onto the treadmill of cool, customers started reaching for their wallets way more frequently than they had before. Take media formats, for example. After music became digital, every physical medium eventually became antiquated. First we said goodbye to records, and soon after to our carefully and expensively curated collection of tapes/CDs/DVDs (except for vinyl lovers, who like to say records "sound warmer," which is just smart enough for me to nod in agreement while having no idea what they are talking about).

Digital music instantly made physically stored music pointless and a nuisance, even if you had spent thousands of dollars building the collection. There's a constant overturning in pursuit of the newest version of something, even when the old version still works fine.

As customers, we quickly adapt to the newest formats, which come with a price tag. We often don't notice this happening, because advertisers have gotten very good at selling it to us without our realizing we're being sold. For example, how did they instill in us the idea that we need the absolute latest smartphone available?

By using pop culture.

Do you remember that Oscar selfie featuring a famous set of faces? At the 2014 Oscars, host Ellen Degeneres snapped a shot on her new phone. The photo, featuring Bradley Cooper, Julia Roberts, Brad Pitt, Channing Tatum, Jennifer Lawrence, and others, was retweeted millions of times.

Do you remember what phone she used to take the shot? People often guess iPhone, making it the cheapest marketing Apple ever got. Because it turns out that Samsung paid $20 million for that "moment" to just sort of "happen."[15]

That spontaneous selfie is an example of something called product integration, where customers see a product used in real life without realizing it's an ad. It's effective because it seems unplanned. Key word being *seems*. There's nothing spontaneous about nine of the most famous people in entertainment all standing at one spot at one time for a picture.

It's a method by which they create an event out of a product release, and then keep doing it. What has followed the Samsung Galaxy S4? The S5, the S6, the S7, and on and on. We're on an upgrade treadmill, and once we know that it's our opportunity to hop off.

An amazing video, *The Story of Stuff*, describes perceived obsolescence this way:

Each of us in the US sees 3,000 advertisements a day. We see more [ads] in one year than people 50 years ago saw in a lifetime. And if you think about it, what's the point of an ad but to make us unhappy with what we already have? So 3,000 times a day we are told our hair is wrong, our clothes are wrong, our car is wrong, we are wrong. Which we can fix by going shopping.

In the US we spend 3 to 4 times as many hours shopping as our counterparts in Europe do. So we're in this ridiculous situation where we go to work, maybe two jobs even, and then we come home, we plop down on our new couch and watch TV, and the commercials tell us "You Suck!" so we have to go to the mall to buy something to feel better and go to work more to pay for the stuff we just bought and then we sit on the couch more and watch more commercials and then we go shopping again…and we're on this crazy Watch-Spend treadmill, and we could just stop.[16]

This is a hamster wheel of chasing stuff, spinning and spinning while getting us nowhere.

THERE'S A MALL IN YOUR POCKET

From the beginning, shopping malls have been designed for exit placement, food court location, direction of corridors, and other uninteresting details to help you go in for a new pair of jeans and come out having bought a pretzel and upgraded your phone plan, too.

But now you don't even have to go to the mall to be in one. Phones put the mall in our pockets, and at our fingertips. Our smartphones are capable of a great many amazing things, and most of those things are connected to spending money. iTunes. Netflix. Free apps that help you function better, but also advertise to you and upsell you along the way.

How did they do it? A generational sales strategy, that's how.

Growing up, I didn't have a mobile phone (I agree, that *does* make me sound 900 years old). I don't miss those days, because without the device, if I didn't know something, I just didn't know it. I had to pretend I did till I could sneak away to look it up.

Here's another one: if you agreed to meet your friends somewhere, and you got there and couldn't find them, you waited for a while and then went home and called them on your house phone.

Holy crap, life is easier with a cellphone.

At the same time, we were fine without them. Honestly. I remember how our lives changed when mobile technology became readily available. Now, in exchange for the increased efficiency, possibility, and connectivity, smartphones interrupt our time for quiet reflection, rewrite our priorities and subtly tip us toward being needy, impatient, and insistent. They allow us to go around "wanting it now," a mentality that is very dangerous to take with you into the store.

Mobile phones are the most quickly adopted consumer technology in the history of the world.[17] As the number of users constantly goes up, so does the societal pressure to adapt or be left behind. In a very short time, we went from a cellphone being an indicator of your wealth to not having one being a symbol of lack of money. We felt greater and greater pressure to have a phone, until it became weird not to have one, or even to entertain the notion that we might not need one. If you've had a phone your whole life, you probably can't imagine what that would be like, which means at this point having a smartphone is effectively a basic human need.

We are the iGeneration.

I read an article a while back about a guy who bought the cheapest iPhone he could get with the cheapest plan he could find. Since you have to take a two-year contract to get the deal, he ended up locked into paying just over $1,000 a year for two years. At the time, that was a lot for a phone. Now for many people it feels normal to pay $1,000 a year for a phone.

A 2012 *Wall Street Journal* article tells the story of Melinda, an accounting clerk at a California high school who pays $300 a month for her family's four smartphones. [18]

Two of the phones have unlimited data, meaning she pays the same price no matter how much she surfs the web. "She has taken advantage of that freedom to watch TV shows such as *Covert Affairs* and *Grey's Anatomy* on her phone almost every day," the article says.

But when she needed to replace her three-year-old smartphones, her carrier announced that unlimited data was not included at the current price. She had effectively developed a streaming habit that cost her and her husband more than $1,000 to maintain via two new high-end phones. Their other option was settling for a tiered-data plan, which could cost her a lot more to indulge her video habit.

"Speed entices more usage," Verizon Chief Financial Officer Fran Shammo said at an investor conference, according to the transcript referenced in the article. "The more data [customers] consume, the more they will have to buy." [19]

There's another interesting example in the article about forty-year-old Scott Boedy, a neighborhood service representative for a cable company. He and his wife pay $200 a month for cellphone service, up by about fifty dollars from the year before. To cover this cost, they had to cut spending on groceries by shopping at discount chains and "fun stuff" like going out to dinner and movies.

"Looking over the family budget on Sunday night, Mr. Boedy said, his wife marveled at how much of it was going to the phone company."

"It stinks," Mr. Boedy said. "I guess it's the cost of modern-day America now."

Automatically paying increased costs should be a choice, but the culture of consumption won't remind you that you have the decision-making power in these situations. You really do. In fact, messaging (a.k.a. advertising) actively obscures your choosing power.

THE ART OF ADVERTISING

Advertising is all around us. Not only this, but every ad we see is the result of a bunch of brilliant, creative marketers sitting around planning and drawing and writing and pondering which description of their product will impress you the most.

It's often for responsible for making us feel inadequate in some way. Consider this scene from the 2002 movie *Roger Dodger*, where high-school-aged Nick visits his uncle Roger at work.

Nick: My mom said you could show me what you do here. So what do you do all day?

Roger: What do I do all day? I sit here and think of ways to make people feel bad.

Nick: I thought you wrote for commercials.

Roger: I do. But you can't sell a product without first making people feel bad.

Nick: Why not?

Roger: (thinks for a second) Because it's a substitution game. You have to remind them that they're missing something from their lives. Everyone's missing something, right?

Nick: Well, yeah. I guess.

Roger: Trust me, they are. And when they're feeling sufficiently incomplete, you convince them that your product is the only thing that can fill the void. So, instead of taking steps to deal with their lives, and instead of working to root out the real reason for their misery, they run out and buy a stupid-looking pair of cargo pants.

Nick: So . . . is it fun?

Roger: It can be.[20]

Yikes. If we really stop and think about it, we start to appreciate the talent we're pitted against. As explained by *Mad Men*'s Don Draper, "I don't 'work in advertising.' I shape society's collective consciousness."[21]

That's consumer society: the most talented and creative people in the game are paid to use their skills to sell you things you don't need and aren't necessarily good for you, because they need to pay their bills, too.

This means the ideal consumer is one who navigates his or her daily life with a certain degree of insecurity about his or herself. If that insecurity is not actually created by advertising, it's a dormant insecurity ads are trying to trigger. Our self-worth issues may derive from any number of reasons, but the cause is not what's important in this case. It's what it makes us do. Our lack of self-worth is accessed and heightened by companies as part of their sales process—it's the first step in convincing us that buying their product will fill that void.

This illustrates how a successful seller blurs the lines between you achieving lasting happiness and you acquiring things that make you happy temporarily.

Advertising is more a part of our culture today than ever, even turning movies into stealthy commercials. We tend to think of TV and movies as merely wish fulfillment, but they're actually powerful engines for generating desires. If they were good for wish fulfillment, they'd actually deliver. Instead, they set to work convincing us how we want to live, how we want to look, how we want to dress, what we want to drive, where we want to travel, what job to strive for. In other words, movies are filled with messages about money.

We've likely all heard of "product placement," wherein companies pay film producers money to feature their product within the story. While product placement started back in 1919, Hershey mainstreamed this move when the company paid a million dollars to have Reese's Pieces featured prominently in 1982's *E. T.*[22]

It's a practice that has only expanded since. The first James Bond film with Daniel Craig—*Casino Royale*—could have been called "CaSONY Royale." On top of that, it showcased something even subtler: purchase placement.

Consider this little scene where Bond reserves a hotel room when his pursuit of a crime ring takes him to the Bahamas.

Clerk: Welcome to the Ocean Club sir. How may I
    help you?

Bond: Yes, I'd like a room please, but it's a spur of the
    moment thing and I haven't got a reservation.

Clerk: We have an ocean view villa available.

Bond: (handing her his card) Perfect.[23]

Wait, what? I feel like something was missing from that conversation. Oh yeah, the price of the room.

I shudder to think how uncool I would have been in the same scenario.

Me: Hold on, how much is it? FOUR THOUSAND
    DOLLARS? A night? Is there a Best Western
    nearby?

I think this scene embodies our fantasy about spending money—not just spending as much as we want, but even managing to look cool as we spend it. It's not cool to look at the price. Think about the times you've split the check at a restaurant with other people. Half of your party acts like they don't care, the rest avoid eye contact because it's uncomfortable. If you want to make sure everything is fair by being the one to do the math, you start wondering if everyone thinks you're cheap.

These expectations we put on ourselves make us feel poorer than we are, and make us feel lame when we're just trying to be smart.

HOLIDAY WARS

Every December in America people tend to talk about the War on Christmas. They worry about what it means that they should say "Happy Holidays" instead of "Merry Christmas." What's missed in this debate is far bigger impact that consumerism is having on the meaning of the holiday.

December 25 is a day of gift giving, and every year the advertisers and social influencers in our lives strengthen the link between love and consumer spending. This link implies if you love your children, your parents, and your friends and family, you'll get them presents. If you don't, you are a Scrooge.

Historically, other than offering treats on holidays, celebrating specific days by buying things for people have almost never been the case. Yet in a capitalist society, religious traditions are often replaced by buying traditions. Slowly and imperceptibly, we redefine the holidays themselves.

Making the decision not to buy presents for family has become revolutionary, and seems to be more about whether or not we care about them than about sticking to our values as consumers.

As a result, the holidays have become a time of year when our feelings around not having enough money collide with feeling that we need to demonstrate our love for the people in our lives by buying them things. It creates a sort of shame cocktail.

Typically every year, reports and videos are released pointing out how much money we spend on presents and how little we give to those in need. One of them reads like this:

"DID YOU KNOW AMERICANS SPEND $450 BILLION ON CHRISTMAS EVERY YEAR? EVERY. YEAR."[24]

OK. First off, wow.

But second, how is that supposed to empower me to give? *I* didn't spend $450 billion on Christmas. So why should I take on the guilt of a spending cycle contributed to by millions of other people? I like what these videos are trying to do, but at the same time, quite honestly, they are really shaming, and not much else. I'm afraid they neither fix our fear around giving, nor deal with the shame of being perceived as not having enough.

It's so much bigger than "buy less stuff."

Every Christmas we try to curb our greed by making ourselves feel bad about it, but that only succeeds in creating intense feelings of shame. The cure for that shame is often (ironically) to go buy more stuff.

Clearly, that's not working.

In reality, the Christmas shopping season has become a chilling example of the comfort people have developed with remaining in debt.

One study found that, in 2010, 13.6 million Americans bought their kids Christmas presents, despite still paying off credit card debt from the Christmas presents they bought an entire year earlier.[25]

The same study also found that, while many Americans say they will struggle to afford Christmas presents, only 36% of Americans say they will set a budget to protect themselves from overspending on the holiday. This is consistent with the national average of budgeters in general. So even though the pressure to spend increases, the unwillingness to set boundaries remains the same.

Consider our average spending per person during the Christmas season over the past decade:[26]

Year	Average spending	Change
2004	$1,004	3%
2005	$942	-6%
2006	$907	-4%
2007	$859	-5%
2008	$431	-50%
2009	$417	- 3%

Year	Average spending	Change
2010	$658	58%
2011	$646	-2%
2012	$854	32%
2013	$801	- 6%
2014	$861	8%

The percentage of change each year declined during the early Iraq War years, and it went down steeply when recession hit in 2008, but spending soared soon after, and had doubled by 2014.

So when did shopping hijack relationships? When did consumption supersede common sense, or even a sense of community? In our culture, the season of Advent has become the season of advertising.

We often find that by the time the actual holiday itself rolls around, we're exhausted. We've spent so much money on presents and been stressed for so much on our time over the past month that we're too drained to really feel close. Then somehow by incredible coincidence, we eat and drink too much, too. Of course, this is connected to guilt as well. It's a season without self-control.

CHAPTER 2 – CULTURE OF CONSUMPTION

THE SHOPPING DEAD

The holiday that actually kicks off the Christmas season is the fourth Friday in November: Black Friday.

Black Friday is the busiest shopping day of the year and the kick off to the holiday shopping season. People line up for hours in advance of store openings, often going out the night before to get a good spot in line. The night before is Black Friday Eve, a wonderful time of the year and a chance to connect as a family—or as it used to be known, *Thanksgiving*.

Thanksgiving used to be a day when you got away from society—when you spent time with family, you got out of the earn-and-spend cycle, and you were thankful for what you had. Now, it's a time when you split your family up to wait in long lines outside Best Buy and anticipate what you're going to spend your money on as soon as those doors open.

We now spend a holiday standing in lines to buy stuff.

That trend only started a few years ago, but some people now wait in line even before Black Friday. An ABC article points that by 2014 people had started lining up as much as three weeks before Black Friday.[27]

The husband of one woman standing in line was quoted as saying, "The point is to get the sales, because everybody is on a fixed income and we don't have that kind of money to splurge." Their goal: a fifty-inch, high-definition TV for $199.

Who has three weeks to put their life on hold so they can stand in line time-after-time in order to buy a TV? A device that itself will only lead to putting a lot more life on hold in the future?

In 2013, many stores started opening their doors on Thanksgiving Day, including Wal-Mart. The holiday devoted to gathering family together is changing rapidly because stores claim to be responding to consumer demand they themselves engineered.

So it's up to us.

Consider this. Do you know why it's called Black Friday? In the early 1960s, Philadelphia police used the term to describe the traffic jams afflicting Philadelphia's downtown shopping district. Hoping to put a better spin on it than "terrible traffic day," retailers tried to rename it "Big" Friday, but that failed to stick. So now they float the notion that it's the day when retailers begin to show a profit—when they're "in the black."[28]

In other words, Black Friday is a holiday for retailers, not for consumers. The biggest gift consumers seem to give during the holiday season is the gift they give to retailers.

So, who is forcing us to do this? We can stop the trend before it gets even worse. We can get back to focusing on Thanksgiving, if we will only choose to. But they're not going to do it for us.

It's safe to say that what happens on Black Friday is a long way away from gratitude for what we have. It's scary. News reports of people actually trampled, stabbed, seriously injured, or even killed. One student told me he worked at a department store where one of the shoppers bit another shopper during a fight over a computer monitor. How scared would you be, knowing that a zombie outbreak was starting in front of your eyes, and that you were about to die in an OfficeMax?

Did you know the first zombie movies were actually written to satirize the effects of consumerism and materialism? In his review of George Romero's 1978 film *Dawn of the Dead*, film essayist Ryan Levin points out that brain-dead mobs of zombies were meant to represent " . . . open-mouthed shoppers wandering through the halls of the temples of capitalism."

"Both are potentially life-threatening, single-minded herds who shamble around with glassy-eyed stares . . . pressing their faces against glass doors and traveling around, hands forward, clamoring for sustenance (brains) and/or those sweet, sweet deals." [29]

I think we can say no to the creepier elements of the Black Friday invasion. We can wake ourselves up. But not by shaming ourselves into better money habits.

We have to know ourselves. We have to understand our relationship to money. Then we can make better choices, and when the time is right, use that money to help others.

So, what to do? First, learn the habit of saving; second, practice the art of contentment.

A SAVING HABIT

America has a saving problem. While Japan's personal savings rate (amount of income saved after expenses) is 40%, Luxembourg's is 17.4%, and Sweden's is 13.4%, America's is 5.3%.[30] Millions of Americans are not getting the full advantage of a habit that really helps you live with less stress and more options.

According to the Organization for Economic Cooperation and Development, the 2008 economic collapse didn't even change this trend. Leading into it, Americans saved on average less than 5% of their disposable income.[31] The collapse and the resulting nervousness and spending decrease raised our savings level to just over 6%. By 2014, it was back down to around 4%.[32]

One of the biggest reasons we don't have a savings culture in the US, when other countries do, is because we stopped nurturing one.

Our attitudes around money run true to patterns from the early twentieth century after World War I. We were in a boom time with unrivaled prosperity, and we spent it rather than saved it. It seemed there was no need to save during the 1920s.

I wonder if anyone felt good about that impulse in the decade that followed? The decade we call the Great Depression. We still struggle to learn this lesson, because despite our economic ups and downs as a country, our savings rate has never rivaled that of other countries.

Over the past three decades, Germany, France, Austria, Belgium, and Sweden have all maintained household saving rates between 10% and 13%. With such high household savings rates, these countries are benefitting from having encouraged their citizens to save for generations. They created hundreds of savings banks and opened easily accessible post office locations for banking. And, not insignificantly, they accepted small deposits. School savings banks were also created.

During both world wars, their citizens were constantly reminded to save their money, while we were told to spend. These European savings campaigns continued long after World War II.

Author Sheldon Garon writes:

All this fostered cultures of saving that endure today in many advanced economies. The French government attracts millions of lower-income and young savers with high-interest savings accounts available at savings banks, postal savings banks and all other banks. These small savers' accounts are tax-free, require only a tiny minimum balance, and commonly pay above-market interest rates. In German cities, one cannot turn the corner without coming upon one of the immensely popular savings banks, called Sparkassen. Legally charged with encouraging the "savings mentality," these banks offer no-fee accounts for the young and sponsor financial education in the schools.[33]

Having been a financial literacy advocate in the U.S. for years, I can tell you that financial institutions, volunteers, associations, and government agencies are doing incredible work across the country. However, financial literacy is struggling to find its momentum as a movement, as well as its way into popular consciousness.

It probably doesn't help that simple, old school money habits are rarely glamorized or celebrated. For most, it's not baked into us from a young age that saving is a crucial step in creating options for ourselves. Instead, we're constantly pressured to spend. In our culture, saving is cutting back on the fun rather than building toward something far more exciting: the capacity to achieve a dream.

CULTIVATING CONTENTMENT

Contentment, what Socrates called 'natural wealth,' is a skill that can't be bought at any price. It is a practice, and it starts with deciding what you really want, not necessarily what other people tell you you're supposed to want. Then it's filling your life with those things, many of which cannot be bought, because many of them aren't things at all.

Let's revisit that "well-dressed businessperson-type," now that we know more about actual millionaires. I was once at a legislative function and was approached by an attorney. Based on his clothes and his confidence, he seemed successful and like he had money. Nice watch. Expensive-looking suit and Italian leather shoes. His tie clip glinted, as did his cufflinks.

I was dressed up for the occasion as well, and he initiated a conversation by complimenting me on my suit.

Attorney: That's a nice suit. I like the three-button style. Yeah, really nice.
Me: Thanks. Actually, I got it at Goodwill for $15.
Attorney: Oh, that's interesting . . .

And then he immediately walked away.

He was right—it was a great suit. But upon telling him where I got it, he left so quickly I didn't get the chance to tell him that $15 is a high-end purchase at Goodwill. You can probably even spend less than that. Someone once paid a lot of money for it, but that someone wasn't me. I have no problem being a second owner. The way I look at it, new to me is still new.

While it was strange to feel devalued by this person, the main conclusion was that we don't have to play by their rules. *We* get to decide where we place our priorities, and where we commit our resources. I happen to believe that what is *within* us is infinitely more important than what is *on* us.

But for many people, this feels like failure.

If you have to ride the bus to work, or shop at secondhand stores, you start feeling like you haven't made it in life. Even if you're making plenty of money, all of a sudden your neighbor buys a nicer car, and—bam—self-doubt.

All this stuff plays into a vulnerability that has nothing to do with money. It speaks to a need we have that is a lot more about feeling valuable than about owning valuable things.

Look, you don't have to announce it in the first five seconds. Certainly, there is some truth to the expression "Money talks." But I'm still trying to figure out what it's saying. Buying things rarely brings you lasting happiness, just momentary bliss. I discovered that I'm perfectly happy shopping at thrift stores and cooking at home instead of going out to eat. Now, I do buy retail and I do go to restaurants. I just make those things occasions rather than everyday occurrences.

If you can develop a lifelong love of getting a good deal, you may realize that expensive things don't make you happier, even in the short term. If you can truly enjoy saving money on your purchase, you'll keep countless extra dollars in your account while still meeting your material needs. Those are dollars you'll have when you really need them.

We can't choose not to be consumers, but we can choose what *kind* of consumers we will be.

In the rest of the book, we'll be looking at three major areas to consider how we can use each one to build a better relationship with money. We'll learn skills in each area that help us move toward health, happiness, and fulfillment.

I mean, if you're into that kind of stuff.

CHAPTER 3:

BUYING TIME

"When you have a few thousand dollars in your checking account, you are mighty."

  – Zac Bissonnette, How to Be Richer, Smarter,
    and Better-looking than Your Parents [34]

MMMMARSHMALLOWS

Let's begin with marshmallows.

In the 1960s, a psychologist named Walter Mischel and a team of researchers at Stanford University created The Marshmallow Test.

It's not the one where you try to put as many marshmallows in your mouth as possible. That's Chubby Bunny. I don't know what that one proves, except that no one looks his or her best when drooling.

The Marshmallow Test was conducted on a group of four-year-old kids, and it yielded absolutely fascinating results. The research team put a group of children, one by one, in a room with a marshmallow. They told the children they could eat the marshmallow whenever they wanted, but if they waited till an adult came back they could eat two marshmallows.

First off, I wasn't aware that psychological experiments could be straight up ADORABLE.

The kids are sitting there, trying not to think about that marshmallow, but you can tell it's their whole world. One kid starts smelling it before putting it down and putting his head in his hands. Another looks away, trying to pass the time, but his fingers creep over and hold onto the marshmallow, as if to reassure him that his sugary prize hasn't up and vanished.

Only a small number of kids could wait. The researchers studied both groups of children throughout their life—the ones who waited and the ones who didn't—and discovered some surprising patterns. The high delayers, those who could wait to eat their marshmallow until the adult came back, were unaffected by a number of risk factors that did affect the low delayers, those who couldn't or didn't wait, or in some cases, didn't even hesitate.

One of the low delayers was a child who seemed to be thinking, "I don't know why you're even telling me the rules. I intend to finish this marshmallow before you leave the room." She didn't say this, but then again, her mouth was full. One of the four-year-olds was able to wait, and looked by the end like a stressed-out 45-year-old.

Here is what the team discovered about those who were able to wait:

- They struggled less in stressful situations.
- They had less trouble paying attention.
- They had less difficulty maintaining friendships.
- They scored higher on the S.A.T. (by over 200 points).
- They struggled less with their weight.
- They struggled less with actual substance abuse problems.[35]

So when I watch this experiment, and read the research that came from it, it's pretty clear that the Marshmallow Test is not just about four-year-olds. It's about us. It's about our ability to control our impulses and hold out for something better.

I cannot think of a more delightful visual for the money in our pockets, our wallets, and on our phones, than the Marshmallow Test. We are in the room. All around us are ways we could easily spend our money.

There's one problem though. This test is often misinterpreted into the message "you just need to have more willpower."

Don't rely on willpower.

Willpower is finite. It runs out gradually as you use it throughout the day. When you have decision-fatigue, you make choices more hastily and you're especially vulnerable to the quick hit of sugar in a candy or soda (conveniently displayed beside you while you wait in the checkout line). One thing to keep in mind is to be wary of making important decisions later in the day.[36]

This experiment has been widely misinterpreted to say that it's all up to willpower, and if we make bad choices, it's our fault and we should stop. This is totally not the point of the experiment. Interviewed on the podcast *Invisibilia*, Walter Mischel shares his big truth in life: "People can use their wonderful brains to think differently about situations, to reframe them, to reconstruct them, to even reconstruct themselves."

When Mischel told the child ahead of time she or he could just pretend that the marshmallow was not really there, the same child would wait fifteen minutes. When the child was empowered to think differently, it dramatically changed the child's behavior."[37]

The key isn't willpower at all; it's to change your environment.

Which kid would you have been? I would have eaten the marshmallow. But that's not going to help any of us win. What will help us win is thinking about the decisions we make, not only in terms of willpower, but also in terms of the environment we are in when we make those decisions.

It turns out you can more easily change your choice by changing your environment. What sights, sounds, and smells are around you when you make a spending decision? Are you hungry? Are you with friends? You can change your environment so that you have other things to focus on beside the thing you want to buy.

Examples of choice environments: your social circle, your exposure to craving triggers, your ability to distract yourself. Things like alcohol, friends, and late-night decision fatigue are choice influencers. That's why some people put their credit card in a block of ice in the freezer.

So when they come home at two o'clock in the morning and decide they want to order an entire pizza, they can't. They already chose wisely, at a time when choosing wisely was way easier. In other words, they pre-decided.

Also in the *Invisibilia* episode, Stanford University psychologist Lee Ross agrees, pointing to the environment as the key factor in predicting decisions.

"People are predictable, that's true, but they're predictable because we see them in situations where their behavior is constrained by that situation, the roles they're occupying, and the relationships they have with us."

So you'll do better by being aware of your environment. Try to avoid shopping when you're bored, angry, sad, with friends, or when you're tired. In these cases, you're combining your fatigue with a variety of emotional environments that will influence your spending. I heard someone say once, "It's easier to keep out than to get out." If you don't go into the store, you are way more likely to not buy anything in that store. And if you spend money online, don't have your credit card information saved so it only takes a click or two to buy. Make it tougher to choose badly and you'll wind up choosing wisely.

SAYING NO TO SAY YES

Saving money is all about being able to say no to ourselves. Every day we are tempted to spend our money on things both big and small, but if we could wait, then down the road we'd have more money to spend on bigger, better, and more meaningful things.

Living in a culture of consumption, we are tested on this all the time. It's an industry of impulse. Whatever you're craving at any moment is a click or tap away. When you live in a consumer culture, having a little money to spend is like being in a room with a marshmallow. More often than not, we're in the room.

When we delay gratification—wait to eat the marshmallow—not only does it pay off in the end, it often pays off more substantially than if we had just gone for instant gratification.

But you don't inherit the ability to delay gratification. You build it by facing this decision over and over again: do we spend more than we can really afford to get the thing we want now, or do we wait? What if we skipped the purchase entirely? Then we'd still have the money with us later on when we need it. And if we skipped the purchase and left the money in an account, over time that money could increase through interest. Eventually we'd have two marshmallows instead of one.

So what is it for you? What is the thing that's really hard for you to resist, even though it would clearly pay off if you could just wait? What's your first marshmallow?

There are two ways to look at it. Either you stop spending money on your marshmallow entirely and try to cut it out of your life, or you acknowledge that it's a reward you genuinely look forward to, and you use it as motivation to cut spending in some other area where you have greater control.

In other words, where will you save in order to splurge?

You're already motivated; you just need to figure out what it is that motivates you. You need to find your second marshmallow. Let's talk about three possible second marshmallows.

Second Marshmallow #1: Values

From a young age, I absorbed the importance of saving money. We've all heard our parents encourage this, and while I may not have listened to much of what they said, seeing how the lack of money affected my family led me to actually follow this piece of advice. Watching my stepfather lose a job showed me that debt takes away options, and often makes life more challenging. So I started saving long before I realized exactly what I wanted to pursue in life. I would only later realize that my built-up habit of saving would become essential to pursuing my dream of writing and speaking.

What are your fears when it comes to money? What's a negative outcome that you've seen in others or experienced for yourself that you want to avoid in your future? Ask yourself, just like I did after meeting my unlikely Scottish reverse-mentor, "What money habits have played a role in bringing these people to this negative spot in their life?" Crosscheck them against your own behaviors, and if they look too familiar for comfort, try to do something differently.

A long-running money habit—also known as a thousand tiny money decisions over time—can impact your life the same way one very large money will. Buying a house can cost you $250,000 in one purchase, but so will raising a child till age 18.[38] Smoking cigarettes over the course of your life will cost you *double* that.[39]

Your money habits need to support what you value most in life.

Second Marshmallow #2: Experiences

Or maybe, like so many of the people I meet in my work, the desire to travel is a powerful motivator for you.

Would you like to travel more, or get started? I love to travel. I've seen Scottish castles, backpacked across Europe, hiked in the rainforests of Puerto Rico, swam in the Mediterranean Sea, and seen African elephants up close. (Too close, in fact.)

But here's the thing: I don't travel because I'm rich, but because I save my money. I set an amount of money each year that I'm willing to spend on travel, and I save until I have enough money to do it. If you're looking for a reason to save money, that might be a pretty great place to start.

When I was backpacking, I spent a few days in Paris, which isn't the most affordable of cities. In looking for a way to reduce my costs, I discovered you could buy day-old baguettes cheaply in most bakeries. I could cut down my food budget pretty substantially by eating these day-olds. A lot of people go to France for the food, but I went to France for, well, France.

I remember sitting on a cobblestone street in Paris eating a day-old baguette while admiring the stunning cityscape. The Eiffel Tower was off in the distance. I thought, "I would absolutely make this trade. I am completely willing to eat a little less pleasurably in order to see new places and have new experiences."

Find your Eiffel Tower, the thing you must see that motivates you to make sacrifices in other categories of your budget. That's the image I want you to hang on to. We don't save money because it's fun. We save money because we have a goal that makes it worth doing.

Are you willing to drive a beat-up car because you want to become a paid musician? Sure. Can you bring your lunch from home because you want to make a difference in the lives of others? Of course. That's how you stick to your budget and control your spending. You sacrifice in one area to better support another area that means even more to you.

What is the goal that is going to give you the discipline and motivation you need? When you find it, it'll snap all this into perfect focus for you.

Second Marshmallow #3: Career Flexibility

Most millennials will have anywhere from ten to fifteen different jobs in their life,[40] which is why the skill we're talking about is so relevant. I had eight before I began my career as a speaker. The crucial advantage you get from saving money is flexibility. This has been especially valuable in my current job, which is one I created for myself, rather than one I was hired for.

I discovered the perfect way to remind myself of the rationale for saving when I saw a Joseph Gordon-Levitt bank-robbing movie called *The Lookout*: "Whoever Has the Money Has the Power."[41]

Power is exactly what saving money creates for us. The power to make decisions we couldn't otherwise make, about our jobs, where we live, how we spend our time, and what we purchase.

You shouldn't rob a bank to make money, but you also shouldn't have to. Saving creates options. Saving is a secret source of autonomy, because every dollar you save is a dollar you have for something more important later on.

BUILD AN EMERGENCY FUND

Did you know the first step for people trying to get out of debt isn't to pay down their debt? It's to save money. Save enough to get through a few weeks or months without having money coming in. Ideally you work up to three to six months of living expenses. This is what's called an emergency fund.

What does this mean in practical terms? It means that, if you don't have an emergency fund, when some unexpected cost arrives in your life, you have to pay for it with a credit card instead of savings. An unfortunate option that only puts you further in debt.

This is where we can reverse the momentum—by picking a number you want to save up to. Here's a question to help you pick your number: what did your last emergency cost you? A friend of mine had to replace a transmission in her car, costing her $2000. Others have lost a job, forcing them to put even more charges on their credit card until they found a new job.

This same habit is the key to career flexibility. Saving could also be called self-insurance. Putting aside enough money to pay for three months of living expenses in case you lose your job is much cheaper than paying for a short-term disability insurance policy year after year. Rather than make payments into a plan that will activate should you lose your job, you could put that money in an account and you'll have it when you need it.

Many millionaires have an emergency fund, but they often take it to the next level, with emergency accounts that cover a year or more of living expenses. With this kind of saving, if they want to make a radical change to their life, they can do it.

That's a pretty striking example of the kind of freedom and leverage that a good amount of savings can lead you to. You don't like your job? You leave your job. You want to travel the world? You travel the world. The money you save allows you to pursue what you want most, rather than preventing you from doing it.

BUYING TIME

By saving money, I bought myself the one thing most people fail to buy themselves in order to pursue their dream: time.

When I was a little kid I thought you saved so you could buy video games. I never thought that saving money would be a tool that would allow me to pursue what I wanted to do with my whole life.

It can be for you, too.

Saving money might just be the most important skill in your arsenal for pursuing the right career, and the right life. Whatever your dream is, it's going to take time. Time to get good at it. Time to meet the people who can give you your opportunity. Time to try other versions of it and quit them if they aren't quite right. Saving money allows you to walk away from the wrong job to make room for the right job. Quitting is scary, but it's a lot less so when you have money saved up to live on.

Your money is your mobility, and saving money is buying time.

BUILD YOUR BATTLE PLAN

Have you ever had fifteen or twenty dollars in your wallet, and you take your wallet out again a few days later, and it's gone? Then you think, "Where did that even go?"

That's a common experience. Buying things is not especially memorable. You're never going to buy a pack of Starburst and say to the cashier, "Can I get a quick picture of you, me, and my Starburst? You know, as a keepsake for my scrapbook?" That is not a moment you will cherish. So you spend the money and don't even remember you spent it.

That's why, if you're going to learn to save, you need to track your spending.

By the way, I gave that example to a group of one hundred high school students once, and when I checked my email later I had five different photos of students posing with cashiers. I sold a lot of Starburst that day, and I laughed and laughed.

When I started budgeting, I learned you're never quite as frugal as you think you are. Color me shocked at the results. In the first three weeks I tracked my spending habits, I discovered I had spent thirty-five dollars on ice cream.

Gross, Colin. That's a rate of almost fifty dollars a month. That's the cost of a phone. That I ate. And it's a lot of ice cream. So there was a place I could make a change.

A budget begins when you make a list of monthly totals in various spending categories (exercise, dining out, phone bill, car insurance, etc.) That's the starting point. The actions you take from there are your chances to take control of your money, your impulses, and your future. Building a budget is how you'll control spending, start saving, track borrowing, identify your income needs, and enable giving.

It's at the heart of this whole book, because self-awareness is the foundation for a healthy relationship with money.

When we budget our expenses, we are quickly faced with a simple choice: change my budget or change my behavior. A budget is essentially a set of boundaries we place on ourselves. We can always break them, but when we do, we know we're living outside a system meant to help us. A budget is not just a bunch of boring numbers. A budget is a way to know ourselves. Either we live within our boundaries, or we don't and we have to live with the increased pressure our boundary-less spending will put on us.

By the way, I know all this cheerleading about budgeting makes me sound very boring. Budgeting *is* boring. Or at least it must be, because only 30% of Americans keep a budget these days.[42] The number was nearer to 40% when I started my job years ago. I don't *think* that decrease is my fault.

Such a low rate is really a shame, because budgeting is one of the most eye-opening and life-changing things I have ever done. Yes, I know how that makes me sound.

Why do only 30% of people budget? One reason is because we tend to think of budgeting as an endless, time-consuming activity. Which isn't actually the case. Once you figure out how to build a budget and put it in place, it will run silently in the background of your life, guiding you and protecting you without filling up nearly as much time as you might think.

The word budget brings up some less-than-pleasant associations, too. The "budget" version of something often means the embarrassingly cheap version. Saying I'm "on a budget" usually comes out apologetically, as a way of explaining that you've run out of money and for a little while at least, the fun is over. It's a limit. It makes you feel as though, unlike everyone else who has enough money not to worry about how they spend it, you have to watch every penny.

But when you think about it in a scheduled manner, you'll actually stress about it a lot less. Budgeting isn't something you do for a season to see how it goes; it should be ongoing, rather than temporary, and you can automate it, so you think about it very rarely. Once you have one, it can keep you from running out of money, which would be far more unpleasant and exhausting.

HOW TO BUILD A BUDGET AND MAKE IT AUTOMATIC

There are lots of resources out there to help you make a budget, and I encourage you to find the one that works best for you.

I struggle with laziness at times, just like anyone else, yet I have been keeping a budget for years now. What's more, I actually like doing it. What's my secret? No big mystery. If you have a credit card or debit card, you have it, too. All you've got to do is go online to websites like www.mint.com or www.ynab.com, or check and see if the credit union or bank where you have an account has online budgeting software. This is a great way to link your card so that any time you use that card it's going to keep track of it.

I use Mint, so when I swipe my debit card at the grocery store, Mint automatically puts the purchase into my Groceries budget. When I reach my allotted total for that spending category for the month, it even sends me an email to let me know.

When you use one of these programs and look at some charts made up of your own behaviors over the past few months, and really see in black and white the moments when your money has gone to stupid things you usually just pretend you didn't buy—well, no big surprise, it really helps you change your behavior.

As for that thirty-five dollars I spent in three weeks on ice cream, well, I didn't just quit eating my favorite dessert because I started budgeting. In fact, I went on to spend another thirty-five dollars on ice cream. Only this time it took me a year.

THE LIFESTYLE PROJECT

In our culture we talk so much about spending and earning, but not about saving. Why are we obsessed with higher salaries and lower costs at the store, but not on saving up to goals that allow a unique lifestyle? One of the great things about budgeting is that it'll help you find out how much you actually need to live the way you like.

Let's put some numbers on this. I'll show you a little project I've done with thousands of students all over New England. I get students to generate a list of the things they will spend money on every month during a year when they are out on their own making those choices—the beginning of being an adult. If their parents are still paying for it—awesome, that's great. That's free to them, at this point. But we still have to count it to put a picture together of what those costs look like. This could be after high school or after college, whenever independence hits.

EXPENSE	MONTH		YEAR
Auto - Fuel	$135	x 12	$1,620
Auto - Insurance	$125	x 12	$1,500
Auto - Payments	$181	x 12	$2,172
Auto - Repairs	$80	x 12	$960
Food - Groceries	$175	x 12	$2,100
Food - Restaurants	$75	x 12	$900
Food - Snacks	$40	x 12	$480
Fun - Going Out	$100	x 12	$1,200

EXPENSE	MONTH		YEAR
Fun - Movies	$25	x 12	$300
Fun - Music	$50	x 12	$600
Health - Exercise	$30	x 12	$360
Health - Hobby	$40	x 12	$480
Health - Insurance	$0	x 12	$0
Health - Travel	$100	x 12	$1,200
Home - Electricity	$50	x 12	$600
Home - Heat	$50	x 12	$600
Home - Internet	$40	x 12	$480
Home - Rent/ Mortgage	$895	x 12	$10,740
Home - TV	$40	x 12	$480
Home - Water	$35	x 12	$420
Misc - Child	$0	x 12	$0
Misc - Clothes	$125	x 12	$1,500
Misc - Coffee	$25	x 12	$300
Misc - Income Taxes	$0	x 12	$0
Misc - Phone	$65	x 12	$780
Misc - Student Loans	$346	x 12	$4,152
Future - Retirement	$50	x 12	$600
Future - Saving	$50	x 12	$600

Looking at some of these numbers, you can see this is not hard science. These are rough averages derived from thousands of high school students' estimates. But what's really informative is the picture that these numbers give us. And this is a legitimate life – paying bills, paying off student loans, even saving for retirement.

Take car payment—typically around $181 per month. If you're spending a lot more than that, you may be putting too much money into the car. If you're spending a lot less, well done. Maybe you bought a used car from a dealer, maybe a junkyard, or I don't know, you just found one somewhere. But you're saving a lot of money each month.

Smartphone? We all have smartphones, so look at that number. Is that right where you're at, or are you way above that? If so, see if you can find a service or plan that gets you down into the $30-$40 per month range. For example, look up MVNO services.

Another great category to discuss is the snacks category. Candy, soda, chips, anything that is convenient and you have to unwrap it. I've seen this number go as high as $150 a month. When you break it down, that's $5 per day. You can see how it adds up. So it's an area where you can really improve what you're spending.

Looking at this list, you may feel a bit depressed. When you buy something small, it's part of a larger pattern with your money, and can add up dramatically over time. Some things I didn't include are student loans, pets, kids, coffee, smoking, and drinking. Actually, they're not here because a lot of the students I talk to are in high school, so we all pretend those are not categories we spend money on. Although one time a student proposed a category called "Chillin'." Which was hilarious. We all knew what he meant.

As I was saying, I did not show you this to depress you, although I may have. I showed you that chart so that I can show you this:

	MONTH	YEAR
Total	$2,927	$35,124

It's the average annual cost of independent life as a young adult.

This is a rough sum of the things you spend money on and the things you like to do. If you look at this number and think it is way too high, the bad news is that it's not going to get a lot lower. Every time I've done this, it's been between $25,000 and $40,000.

Don't worry; I'm not going to leave you in this sad place. Go back and look at some of these categories, so you can form a plan of attack. (This is that part of the book where the author asks you to pause and do something. And if you're like me, you'll keep on reading. But since it really will be so much more useful if you personalize this, I'll help you out by stopping the book.)

There, I stopped. Don't go on till you've tried this.

EXPENSE	MONTH	YEAR
Auto - Fuel	x 12	
Auto - Insurance	x 12	
Auto - Payments	x 12	
Auto - Repairs	x 12	
Food - Groceries	x 12	
Food - Restaurants	x 12	
Food - Snacks	x 12	
Fun - Going Out	x 12	
Fun - Movies	x 12	
Fun - Music	x 12	
Health - Exercise	x 12	
Health - Hobby	x 12	
Health - Insurance	x 12	

EXPENSE	MONTH	YEAR
Health - Travel	x 12	
Home - Electricity	x 12	
Home - Heat	x 12	
Home - Internet	x 12	
Home - Rent/ Mortgage	x 12	
Home - TV	x 12	
Home - Water	x 12	
Misc - Child	x 12	
Misc - Clothes	x 12	
Misc - Coffee	x 12	
Misc - Income Taxes	x 12	
Misc - Phone	x 12	
Misc - Student Loans	x 12	
Future - Retirement	x 12	
Future - Saving	x 12	

Total	x 12	

Nice! Now that you've done that, let me show you lots of ways to adjust your actions to lower that total number.

SCRAPE SEASON

A scrape season is when you shut down your expenses for a short time so you can reverse the momentum on your financial situation. The bad news is you will have to make some sacrifices. The good news is this will not last forever.

Your scrape season may end up being a few weeks or months. It might work a lot faster than you think, and the initial sacrifice might lead to a journey that's much more rewarding than you expected.

Here's an amazing story from Laura, a teacher who heard me speak to a student audience and thought, "I want some financial freedom in my life, too." Here's how Laura delivered herself from debt. Listen to the language she uses to describe her starting point:

> At the time I was $10,000 in credit card debt and I was *frustrated* because every bit of money I had was going toward paying bills and *I felt like I was never going to be able to climb out of debt.* I was too *embarrassed* to tell my husband about my debt, and I was *nervous* about taking out loans for my son for his first year of college. And my other son was looking

at another similarly high-priced college. So, *I was just churning and churning and not going anywhere!*

Laura was $10,000 in debt—$4,000 debt on a credit card at 20% interest ($80/month in just interest), and $6,000 debt at 17% interest on another credit card ($90+/month in interest). She was paying $170-$200 per month in interest alone, and paying her debt off by $1,000/month (but really it was more like $800/month toward the principal). Lastly she was spending $1,000/month (adding an extra $20 each month in interest).

Laura got debt-free in one year. Here's how:

She Stopped Increasing Debt
- Switched all her credit cards (at a $200 penalty) to one card at 0% interest for 18 months.
- Put credit cards away where she couldn't use them.
- Included her kids in her plan by telling them "I need your help to save for your college."
- Used coupons for groceries.
- Used a Rite Aid card for 20% off every purchase.

She Built an Emergency Fund
- Deposited $1,000 per month in an account in a different town, where she couldn't get to it. One of the ways she did this was by saving and

depositing every $5 bill she got (with a target of $100 a month, and eventually added up to $1,400 in a year). She would drive to the other town to make her deposits, so it felt like a celebration.

- Once she was debt-free, she kept this going until she'd saved $6,000 in a separate account.

She Started Controlling Spending
- Created a budget.
- Didn't use a debit card (since she didn't trust herself).
- Gave up her daily soda and morning Starbucks coffee ($5-10/day).
- Started using a water bottle instead.
- Packed lunch from home (saving $4/day).
- Stopped her after-work snack run ($8/day).

(These last three alone saved her $22/day, or $5,720/year).

Now listen to the language she uses to talk about how she feels at the end of her scrape season:

Now that I am not only debt-free, but I have money in the bank, I am *excited* about *my new debt-free financial life*. I am *excited that I can help out my kids with college* and to know that *I will have the means* to do so. I am also excited to realize that *if I want to take a vacation, I can,* without going into debt. And, *I am excited to buy some new clothes*! It has been over a year since I have had new anything!

Laura's story is pretty amazing. She obviously had a lot of self-discipline she didn't know about, and just needed a nudge. A goal. That's often really helpful. Start with a goal. Pick an amount of money you want to save, or an amount of time you want use to really change your habits.

This will be your scrape season, and it's only for a season.

Here are some tips from Jean Chatsky's *Money Rules* to apply as you try this:

- No impulse buying. The best cost-cutting tool is to wait one day to buy something new. If you still want it after one day, go ahead (if you can afford it). If in one day, you've changed your mind, you just saved yourself money!
- Don't shop angry. Anger makes you more optimistic, less concerned about risk.
- Don't shop sad. Research shows sadness makes you eager to buy just about anything. Sadness feels like a big hole you want to fill up.
- Don't shop hungry. This is why stores offer samples: making you drool makes you spend more

money on not just food, but everything. It primes the same part of your brain that responds to the rewards you really want. Alcohol does this, too, while also reducing impulse-control.

- Shop with cheapskates. Our friends influence how much we spend. Dessert. Snacks. Entertainment. Don't shop with constant shoppers.
- Don't budget while you're dieting. Don't diet while you're budgeting. Willpower isn't unlimited. Beware "ego depletion": the lapse of willpower when you're trying too hard to control yourself. Don't work on multiple things that require great willpower. Prioritize them and take them in turn." [43]

Other things to keep in mind:

Plan ahead, and avoid convenience stores. A pint of orange juice is around $2-$3 in a grocery store. It can be $4-$5 in a convenience store. (Sometimes you can get a good deal on a gallon of milk at convenience stores though, so be sure to price-compare.)

Buy your clothes used from thrift stores or clearance racks. A t-shirt in a thrift store will often cost you less than $10, whereas new it might not sell for less than $15 or more. On clearance racks, you can pick up that t-shirt marked down so many times, it might be only a couple of bucks. Really smart shoppers have a saying: "Never pay retail." They also know the price on seasonal clothing when it first shows up on the rack is *not* the real price. The real price is what they mark it down to once the season arrives.

Most people are brand loyal. They always look for names like Apple, Adidas, or American Eagle. This tends to take the focus off cost. Try being price loyal. Look for the inexpensive option, as long as it doesn't compromise the quality.

WAYS TO SAVE

I'm assuming you eat food. If so, consider limiting restaurant trips to once a week, or even once a month, if you can do it.

If you went out to a restaurant and got just a basic meal for one person, nothing fancy, you'd probably spend around $10 for lunch. If you went to a grocery store, do you know how many peanut butter and jelly sandwiches you could make for $10? Same amount of money for the meal, except now you're buying ingredients to make peanut butter and jelly sandwiches. The answer, dear reader, is 22 peanut butter and jelly sandwiches. Think about that. That is an amazing amount of food to make for the same amount of money as one lunch in a restaurant.

What about dinner? Spaghetti. Do you know how many spaghetti dinners you can make for $10? The answer is 12. Twelve spaghetti dinners for $10—that is so much spaghetti.

Now we've covered lunch and we've covered dinner. Now what about breakfast? Do you know how many Cream of Wheat breakfasts you can make for only $10? The answer is a lot. 44! That is so much food!

That would be such great news if Cream of Wheat wasn't disgusting.

Seriously though, if you like it or could learn to like it (totally possible!), then this is an amazing way to make a lot of food for a small amount of money.

Now to be clear, I'm not advising you to eat only peanut butter and jelly and Cream of Wheat for the rest of your life. No. That is not life. That is prison. But I am asking you this: can you spend less on going out to eat, and put the money you save in a bank account instead? Making this switch will begin setting you up for the next chapter of your life.

While they are cheaper, I cannot fully endorse empty-calorie, high-carbohydrate meals. There are plenty of other healthy, nutritious foods that you can buy and prepare meals with that are cheap, that will go far, and are probably a little easier on the digestive system.

Sure, $10 could buy you nine burgers on the McDonald's Value Menu. But soon you may be asking, *What have I done to myself?* And for those people who tend to suggest Ramen noodles, because you can make almost 50 dinners for $10 worth of Ramen noodles, you'll need to factor in future health care costs from giving yourself heart disease in a hurry.

If you are in school, you are in a perfect place to answer the question of what you can add to your $10 menu.

Consider applying this strategy to what you choose to drive and eventually where you choose to live. Learn to ask yourself, "What is something that I do on a daily basis that costs me money, and can I do anything to spend less money and end up with the same result?"

EARNING BY SAVING

Here are ways you can create another source of income for yourself by saving:

- Do not eat out more than a few times per month.
- Skip the PB&J and go with a deli-style sandwich:
  Loaf of bread = $3.00 (16 slices)
  Turkey = $4.00
  Mayo = $3.50
  Lettuce = $1.50
  Cheese = $3.50

If you figure a loaf of bread has 16 slices, then you can make 8 sandwiches for 15.50. Those same 8 sandwiches would cost more than $40 at a deli. So you have just saved $24.50.

- Don't buy a drink with your meal. Drink water. You'll save $1 or $2 every time you do so, and we usually don't drink enough water anyway.
- Fruit/vegetable smoothies are truly delicious. If you have a blender, you can make 10 smoothies for $10:

3 Bananas: $1.00

1 Apples: $1.00

Frozen berries: $3

2 cups Spinach $1.50

Cayenne pepper: $.50

Honey: $3

That's $1 per smoothie. Plus it's a very healthy way to start your day. Make one, tell your friends about it, and experience the weird combination of feeling great while also being instantly annoying to everyone around you.

START SMALL, REALLY SMALL

My friend likes to say, "It's the start that stops most people." So start as small as you have to, as long as you start.

Do you save change?

The first really easy way to build up some money is to cut a slot in a plastic soda bottle and start filling it with loose change. Put the silver coins in, too, not just copper. It'll take a long time, but when it is full, you'll probably have more than $50 in that thing.

There's no reason not to do it. I asked a high school freshman if he saved his change. He said, "I hate change. I just throw it away!" Yikes. But if you know this guy, or someone like this guy, then follow him around.

Oh, wait, not in a creepy way. On second thought, don't.

Also, many bank and credit unions have coin counting machines that you can use for free if you have an account there. You don't need coin-counting machines like Coinstar that take 10% of your money.

But bottom line: just start.

OPEN AN ACCOUNT

Here are a few reasons why I believe everyone should have a bank account:

1) I once spoke at an assembly of 250 students, and I asked if anyone kept their money in their mattress. One girl spoke up and said she kept it in a shoebox. I asked where in her room the shoebox was, and without thinking she replied, "It's under

my dresser." Now 249 people know exactly where her money is kept. Don't do that. If you start an account, your money is safe from theft.

2) With an account, you are now able to get your coins counted for free. No more paying Coinstar a fee to do it.

3) When you have an account, you now can get free financial advice. Many adults pay someone to give them financial advice. If you have an account at a bank or a credit union, you can sit down with a counselor and ask questions, for free, about the best ways to save your money. (Just make sure to ask them if they are a fiduciary, meaning they are obligated to give you advice that benefits you, not only them.)

So a savings account is a free resource that can help you make sense of your money? Sounds well worth it to me.

If you can spend less money on things you need, avoid scams that try to steal from your personal economy, and start thinking like a millionaire, then you will keep a lot of money that otherwise would be frittered away.

So what do we do with the extra money?

Your main options are banks and credit unions.

Generally, we're pretty familiar with banks. We have phrases like "bank on it . . . take it to the bank . . . making bank." Basically, a bank is a business that holds your money for you. It makes a profit by investing the money it has gathered from many account holders, putting it to work in a variety of other financial endeavors. It pays this profit to the people who own shares of stock in the bank.

A credit union, for practical purposes, is similar. It is another financial institution that holds onto your money for you and is equally safe and equally secure (both federally insure your account up to $250,000). A credit union is built on the co-operative model, so if you have money in there, you are considered a part owner. Usually, credit unions try to return the profits to account holders by lowering fees or reducing interest rates charged.

There are also more and more mobile banks and digital account sources for you to consider.

If you're keeping your money in a shoebox or in a mattress, a lot of things could work against you. You could have a fire. A shoebox is easier to rob than a secure building. (Plus your money is insured, meaning you still get it back if your bank is actually robbed. This offer does not apply to the shoebox.)

You want to put your money somewhere it's safe. Not only that, but you want to put your money somewhere where it can start to accumulate interest, to grow, and to reach an amount you really can use.

Banks and credit unions offer savings and checking accounts, certificates of deposit (CDs), and debit and credit cards. These are all services that are often free, so make sure you understand how they benefit both you and the company offering them to you. As I mentioned earlier, banks and credit unions offer you free advice. This is because they want to build a relationship with you, in the hopes that you will go to them when you need a loan to lease a car, buy a house, or start your own business.

Are you Capable or Excluded? According to a 2015 University of Kansas study, using data from the 2014 Financial Capability Study, not having an account of any kind is one of the two factors used to determine if you are Financially Capable or Financial Excluded. Millennials are considered Financially Capable if they have some financial education and a savings account, while millennials are considered Financially Excluded if they have no financial education and no savings account.[44]

Here is why this matters: Financially Excluded millennials are 30% more likely to carry credit card debt, 21% more likely to use financial services that are not federally insured, 176% less likely to be able to come up with $2,000 quickly, and 224% less likely to save for emergencies.

In short, they are on a financial tightrope. And rather than falling, they can safely exit the rope by seeking financial education and opening an account. We can always do better than the shoebox.

START A MOVEMENT

When you decide to get back in shape, or if you want to get in shape for the first time—whenever you start building any habit you're trying to make a regular thing—it helps to buddy up. The same is true with saving money.

Find friends, mentors, and resources to back you up. Without having your friends on the same page, you're going to feel cheap all the time, and isolated by your thriftiness. You'll find it hard to resist overspending again, since it's more comfortable in the freely-spending circle.

But you decide who is in your circle. Do yourself (and your friends) a favor and recruit a few people into your circle who won't give you a hard time for not spending a lot of money. Encourage your peers to make budgets and figure out ways to have good times with less spending. Who knows what might happen? You might just start a movement.

CHAPTER 4:

DEFEATING DEBT

"*The only reason a great many Americans don't own an elephant is that they have never been offered an elephant for a dollar down and easy weekly payments.*"

– *Mad Magazine*[45]

"*I'm Stanley Johnson. I've got a four-bedroom house in a great community. Like my car? It's new. I even belong to the local golf club. How do I do it? I'm in debt up to eyeballs . . . Somebody help me.*"

– *"Perfect Life" Commercial*

In a hyper-consumption society, not only are you pressured to spend more money than you actually have, you can actually do it.

One day I talked with I asked some high school sophomores about school, about life, and then this:

"If I gave you a credit card with a limit of $5,000, what would you spend it on?"

They said:

- "I'd probably buy shoes, encrusted with diamonds. And in the sunlight they'd glisten."
- "I would look for something that costs exactly $5,000."
- "I'd actually have to give the $5,000 to my parents. I'm in a little bit of debt."

My sixth and final subject, Dana, gave me the answer I was looking for: "I'd wait till I'd saved up until I actually *had* the money to spend."

I honestly didn't realize that only one of the six sophomores would answer my question right. Dana understood that debt comes with pretty significant strings attached. The other five were only too happy to dream up what they'd spend the money on (and fair enough), while Dana knew to ask herself, "If I need to borrow it, can I really afford it?"

That's a simple enough lesson, but it's a lesson most of us don't get before getting into our first serious debt. There's even a movie about it.

SHOPAHOLICS ANONYMOUS

As a guy, I should not have even heard of the movie *Confessions of a Shopaholic*, let alone watched it. Admittedly, I'm not the target audience. I've never seen a handbag that I absolutely had to have. It may be a pretty standard romantic comedy, but it tackles a subject movies rarely do: the way spending money can medicate other problems.

In the movie, Rebecca Bloomwood is a shopaholic. Mannequins in store windows call out to her, and she's used countless credit cards to satisfy for her consumer urges. It's quickly catching up with her.

She ends up cornered by a debt collector on live television in front of a studio audience (hats off to Hollywood for finding a way to make a boring, over-the-phone conversation a lot more dramatic and cinematic). What makes things trickier is that Rebecca is now a personal finance reporter. When she's called out, the hypocrisy and shame of the moment cause her to run out of the studio, followed by her enraged boss (who, because this is a romantic comedy, is adorable, age-appropriate and speaks with an accent). He demands she explain her lying and why she's in such terrible credit card debt.

She says, "When I shop, the world gets better, and the world is better, but then it's not, and I need to do it again."[46]

Rebecca stares directly into the camera with the saddest look you've ever seen. It makes you want to adopt a puppy. It's a line that actually does a good job expressing the struggle behind something we call "retail therapy." You know, when you're having a lousy day so you go buy something and feel better. If emotions led you into that store, they'll definitely influence what you do there.

You know that feeling you get when you're wearing a new shirt or a new pair of jeans, and you want people to notice? You feel new. That's the danger right there. Because you're paying money for a feeling, and you'd be better off figuring out how to activate that feeling on your own.

Once after a workshop a student wrote me a letter, and her words, not mine, should convince you this is real:

When you brought up the movie Confessions of a Shopaholic, just about all of the girls in the classroom looked at me. I realized in that moment that I am addicted to shopping. I have to spend the money that's in my pocket, and when I do, it's bliss. I've got that beautiful new purchase in my hand and I am so happy. And then I look at what I have, and I'm disappointed that it's not more, and then I realize that I can't buy any more because I'm broke. Once I realize this, I become sad and feel as though I need more to make me happy again. It's scary to realize I'm addicted, but it's even scarier to know nobody takes this kind of addiction seriously.

If you connect with this, let me be clear—that's OK. In fact, it's great, because now you're aware of it.

If you start right now, you have so much time to change your habits and your psychology around spending. As a start, set yourself a spending limit on one category of shopping, and then begin to practice holding to that limit. Get used to what it feels like to say no internally, and what thoughts and feelings it brings up. The reality is that with addictions, there is usually a physical component to it because the dopamine produced by that euphoric high of buying something is very powerful. So find accountability, get a therapist, and above all be kind to yourself when you mess up.

Give yourself a chance to succeed by reducing the time you spend in a retail environment (this may include not working in one), and take your business to thrift stores and clearance racks. But even there, stick to your pre-decided spending limits.

Pay attention to how much you're saving whenever you find a deal. Write those numbers down so you can feel good about them. Schedule opportunities to make small purchases that you can look forward to. It's so healthy to occasionally pause and reward yourself for your overall improvement. Don't discard 'pretty good' in favor of perfect; you'll only end up blaming yourself when you fail. Instead, focus on slowly changing your behavior for the better over time.

You will change. You will beat this. Choose to.

TAKING OUT LOANS

Here are some of the main types of loans available to you:

There's a mortgage, which is, of course, a loan on a house: this is often a fifteen- or thirty-year commitment to pay back several hundred thousand dollars. Then there is a car loan, where you borrow the money to buy the car and pay it back in monthly installments. You can also get personal loans, student loans, or specialized loans for specific circumstances (bridge loans, small business loans, commercial loans, payday loans, etc.) Payday loans, just in case you've heard this term before, are short-term loans you get by using your next paycheck as a guarantee for the loan. So if you can't pay, you forfeit your paycheck. Also payday loans have notoriously high interest rates and grow progressively harder to pay off the more time goes by. In other words: avoid, avoid, avoid.

OK, so let's say you apply for a loan. What are the things you will need in order to be approved?

- You'll need your driver's license and your social security number. Often, lenders will use this information to run a credit report, looking for a good credit score. If you don't have a good score and they decide to approve you anyway, they'll probably raise your interest rate. So, if you have good credit, that'll be when you thank yourself for doing some of the smart things we talked about.

- Lenders also want to know that you are able to repay the money. They'll want to know your employment history. Do you have recent pay stubs, a current paycheck, and tax information? Are you a stable candidate for that loan?

- They also want to know that if you have borrowed in the past, you have paid it off. Because credit is about how credible and trustworthy you are.

Loans are not the only type of debt to understand. There's the ever-popular credit card to look at, too.

GETTING CREDIT

A simple example of how we use credit is your cell phone. A company gives you a phone to use, and trusts that at the end of the month, you are going to pay them the money you owe. Credit is trust between a lender and a borrower—in this case you're the borrower—and that trust is measured in money: more trust = good credit; less trust = bad credit.

Building good credit is a huge part of our financial lives. It's part of our perceived value when it comes to applying for a loan or a credit card.

One of the most important areas where we have to practice self-control is with credit. In the Lending Tree commercial "Perfect Life," a wealthy-looking man addresses the camera. "I'm Stanley Johnson. I've got a four-bedroom house in a great community. Like my car? It's new. I even belong to the local golf club. How do I do it? I'm in debt up to eyeballs . . . Somebody help me."[47]

Doesn't that just *feel* true?

The essential part of the story we must tell ourselves is this: the "rich" person with the new car and nice house may be—more often than you'd guess—stressed about how she or he will actually be able to pay for those things. They may sit and ask themselves, "How did I get myself into this mess?"

One of the main ways this happens is by getting credit cards without actually understanding how credit works.

As a kid, I remember one of my friends got really into magic. He would spend hours practicing tricks, like scarves that never ended, ropes whose knots would vanish without explanation, and coins he'd make disappear and then reappear behind your ear. It may have been a little odd to have a friend so into magic, but it was worth it when I got to see him leave people speechless.

He helped me see there were three keys: practice, misdirection, and a willing audience. To make the trick work, he would get your eyes off the hand doing the trick for a second and onto something else—misdirect your attention. This works because we want to believe in magic. The stage is set for the young, aspiring magician, because people want to be tricked.

Adults, of course, tend not to believe in magic. Except for when they do. Except for when they put their trust in the magic of credit. Which, just like my friend's disappearing quarter, relies heavily on misdirection. That's the lenders' magic trick. They take your eyes off the number that matters, and refocus your attention on some arbitrary number. While they're doing so, they're actually increasing the number that matters.

"Do you want a $45,000 BMW for only $250 a month?"

Never mind how many months you'll be paying that $250. Or how big a chunk of those payments will be chalked up to interest (profit for the lender) as opposed to paying down the debt itself. The $250 is what you think about; the $45,000 has actually become an afterthought.

This kind of misdirection is the best trick there is because you want to believe you can have what you want and pay for it just a little at a time.

WHEN YOU PAY LATER

Every time you use a credit card you borrow money, and if you carry that balance for more than a month, then you are charged a very small fee called interest. This very small fee is one of the major ways credit card companies make money. You're charged this fee over again every month on any of the money you haven't yet paid back.

The message of a credit card is: "Hey, you don't have enough money for this flat screen TV? No problem! Swipe this card and you can have the TV now. You can *always* pay for it later!"

Obviously, that's a very appealing message.

But here is a simple truth about credit cards: when you pay later, you pay more. Credit card companies make money by loaning you money and then charging you interest over and over, month after month, until you pay it back.

More than a few studies have shown us that credit cards increase spending.[48] A study by Dun & Bradstreet found that people spend 12-18% more when using credit cards instead of cash. The average McDonald's credit card purchase is $7, while the cash average is

$4.50.[49] When we don't figure in the interest at the start, we think we bought something for one price when we'll actually pay more later.

When we pay later, we pay more, and what's in the 'more' category is profit for the credit card companies and a loss for us. Most credit card companies use an APR, or Annual Percentage Rate (a "Compound Interest" formula where the amount you owe is charged an additional 1/12 of your annual interest rate. This means that if you don't pay it off right away you could end up paying 'interest on your interest.'

Let's say you buy something for $1,000. Assuming an interest rate of 15%, and you make no more charges on that card, it will take you 9 years and 10 months to pay back $1,000 in minimum monthly installments. By the time you're done, you will have paid $1,851.03 ($851.03 in interest). What?!

For every single one of your monthly payments, you will pay more in interest than to your actual debt. Take a look at the breakdown of some of these amounts: the first 3 months, year 1, year 2, year 5, and your last payment.

Month	Minimum payment	Interest paid	Principal paid	Remaining balance
1	$20.00	$12.50	$7.50	$992.50
2	$19.85	$12.41	$7.44	$985.06
3	$19.70	$12.31	$7.39	$977.67
12	$18.41	$11.51	$6.90	$913.63
24	$16.82	$10.51	$6.31	$834.70
60	$15.00	$7.72	$4.63	$610.13
118	$2.56	$0.03	$0.02	$0.00

This was computed using http://www.bankrate.com/
calculators/managing-debt/minimum-payment-calcu-
lator.aspx. After five years of faithful payments, you still
owe more than $600 on a $1,000 loan!

So if you use a credit card, you should pay back as
much of the full balance each month as you can to avoid
or greatly limit your interest charges.

When dealing with credit and handling credit cards,
remember Dana's philosophy: "If I have to borrow it,
maybe I can't afford it." At the same time, credit cards
can be useful if you use them wisely. The best way to
build credit worthiness safely is to use a credit card only
after you have the money saved up already. If you want to
buy a flat screen TV, you can. First save up a few hundred
dollars, then buy it on a credit card and get the reward

points, mileage points—whatever they might be offering—and pay it off immediately. This way, you reduce your chance of interest and most importantly, you create a prompt payment record, decreasing your chance of hurting your credit or getting in over your head.

YOUR CREDIT IS YOUR CREDIBILITY

Imagine you are on a playground and you see this guy who has just arm-wrestled five dudes. He's done great—five out of five. They're all lying on the ground and they're crying. Grown men. Crying. He motions to you and as you get closer you can see he's got a scar over one eye and prison tattoos that he gave to himself, probably.

He says to you (in a gravelly, Vin Diesel kind of voice), "We're going to arm-wrestle and you're going to lose."

What do you do?

I'll leave that question up to you. Maybe you're the kind of person that can't back down—it's like a pride thing for you. You're going to wrestle him even though you'll probably end up crying, too. But even if you take on the challenge, all of us would believe his claim that he is great at arm-wrestling. Why? Because he's got the history to prove it. You've seen it. He has credibility.

The same is true with credit. When you fill out a credit card application or ask a financial institution for a loan, your credit standing backs up your claim when you say, "I am capable of paying this money back." Your credit tells lenders that they'll get back the money they loan you, because you've got the history to prove it.

Your credit is your credibility. It's how much people trust you. It's how much they believe you are capable of doing what you claim. That guy on the playground has credibility. You believe his claim. So you need to create your own credibility in order to use credit well, in order to get access to credit cards and to loans.

The best way to do that is by building a credit history that speaks on your behalf.

IMPROVING THE PICTURE

To boost your score, build credit by acquiring and positively managing small lines of credit (like small loans from financial institutions that you pay off quickly), and pay your credit card in full every month.

Did you know that 35% of your credit score is based on any late payments that appear on your credit report? You can't change the past, but you can change your future past by avoiding having to make additional late payments.

Another key to increasing your score comes from understanding a little thing called debt-to-credit ratio. It's simply your credit balance divided by your credit limit.

To manage this to your benefit, you want your credit card balance to be no more than 30% of the limit on the card—or even less—to paint the best possible picture of yourself.

Let's look at one scenario and a plan to improve it. Say you have:

Card 1: $5,000 balance/$10,000 limit = 50 percent debt-to-credit ratio.

Card 2: $4,500 balance/$5,000 limit = 90 percent debt-to-credit ratio.

First, STOP using the credit cards as soon as possible. New debt will only make this tougher to pay off. So, live on your available income to the best of your ability.

Now begin by paying a little extra every month to bring down the principal amount (the actual debt) on the card that is closest to the credit limit (paying more than just minimums lets more money go to paying down the actual debt itself). When you've reduced that card's outstanding balance (the amount you still owe), then move on to the second card that's close to the limit.

In the scenario above, you will want to start with card #2. To get your debt-to-credit ratio down to 30% of the limit, you need to reduce the balance to $1,500. Then you will hold the line with that card and move on to card #1. Pay whatever extra you can afford on that one, bringing it down to $3,000, which is 30% of the card's limit.

Since we only have so much money to work with, this is a good strategy to increase your credit score, access credit, and make the important purchase you want to make.

REASONS TO BUILD CREDIT

The solution to credit problems is not as simple as some advisers claim on TV, where they cut credit cards with scissors and everybody cheers. I think that's a little extreme, although no doubt very satisfying.

Good credit will help you buy a house. You pay for a house with a thirty-year loan and the interest rate that you're charged every month is based on your trustworthiness, your credit rating, and your credibility. This is also the case when buying a car, on a smaller scale in terms of time and cost. The bank or financing agency is going to run your credit history to make sure you are a safe person to loan the money to so you can buy the car.

Be aware of recent trends, like having your credit run by employers when you apply for a job, or run by companies when you sign up for a phone contract, and run by landlords when you rent an apartment.

So credit is something we can't just ignore.

The advantages of having credit cards:

- Establishes a positive credit history if used appropriately.

- Is safer for shopping online than using a debit card.
- Convenient payment tool.
- Useful for emergencies.
- Spreads out payments for big ticket purchases (although if you need to do this you can help yourself out by saving more).
- Protects against fraud.

REASONS TO HANDLE WITH CAUTION

While credit cards are a useful tool, they also make it easy to get into debt and tough to get back out.

The single greatest threat to our personal economies, to our financial futures, and even the direction of our lives, is the way we handle credit cards.

I wish I could say that sentence was needlessly dramatic. (It might be dramatic, but hopefully not needlessly.) If you're wondering how serious an effect debt can have on the rest of our lives, feel free to Google the phrase "credit card stories" sometime. Too many people accept credit cards at face value, not realizing the fine print can trip them up. Those hidden realities come to the surface eventually.

The reason a credit card is so dangerous is because it is a direct path into debt. By its very nature, the minute you purchase something on a credit card, you are in debt until you pay it off. But credit cards are also loaded with ways to drag you further into debt.

Some cards encourage you to spend more money by offering reward points if you spend more. They also offer cash advances, where you withdraw cash at the checkout register or at an ATM. It's basically a very small loan. But did you know that the interest rate on cash advances is much higher than the interest rate on your regular credit card purchases? A friend of mine has a card with a cash-advance interest rate nearly double the interest rate on purchases.

Once you are in debt to a card company, credit cards try to keep you there. Let's talk about a major trick built into every credit card, using an example I found on a coworker's credit card bill. (Even as I say that, I feel I should explain that I had her permission, because that seems incredibly sketchy. I wasn't just hanging out in her office scanning her confidential documents.)

On her bill, as with a lot of bills, there was a white page with black text, and an eye-catching black box containing white text highlighting something called the "minimum amount due."

The minimum amount due (or minimum payment) is the smallest amount that you are legally required to pay each month on the debt that you owe to that company. It's typically equal to 2% of your current debt. So in this case she spent $4,400 using a credit card at an interest rate of 13.24%, and she only has to pay $89 that month. What a great deal, right? Just ninety bucks covers the $4,400 she spent. It's practically free money. Or is it?

According to legislation passed in 2009, the lending industry now has something called the "minimum payment warning" that borrowers are entitled to know. That's where they tell you, "Hey, if you already spent $4,400, and you don't make any more purchases on your credit card ever, and you pay that $4,400 off in minimum payments alone, it will take you twenty-one years to be debt-free."

Think about that: twenty-one years from now, when you are effectively a whole other person in a different stage of your life, you think, "Finally, my last payment!" Add up what you paid back, and you realize that you have spent almost $9,000 ($8,863). All that extra money is interest, and all that interest is profit for the credit card company.

If you did this, not only would you have paid double what you owed, but also according to how credit card interest and repayment are computed, most of your monthly payment on the debt would have gone towards paying off the interest, with far less actually paying down the debt. Even if you wanted to pay it off in one big chunk down the road, most of that initial $4,400 you borrowed would still be sitting there for you to pay off.

"Minimum payments, maximum damage."

I hope you will remember that phrase, and not just because it sounds like a tag line for a terrible action movie. Make sure that movie doesn't end up being about you. Avoid those minimum payments, and you'll avoid the damage that comes with them of paying far more than you ever intended.

The disadvantages of having credit cards:

- May carry additional penalty fees.
- Tempt you to overspend.
- Put you at risk of identity theft.
- Make you responsible for lost/stolen cards (although in many instances credit cards offer important protections).
- Carry costly interest hikes when a balance is past due.
- Base your interest rate on your payment history.

CREDIT REPORTS AND CREDIT SCORES

When a lender checks your credit history, or when you decide you want to check it, that history takes two forms: your credit score and your credit report.

A *credit score* is a numerical summary of the information on your credit report. On a FICO (Fair Isaac Corporation) scale, it's a number between 300 up to 850 that tells you how good your credit standing is (higher is better). It often determines what kind of interest rate lenders will offer you. The higher your credit score, the lower your interest rate.

A *credit report* goes a little deeper. You can run the report on yourself, and it gives you a sense of how you managed your debt in the past.

This is what lenders learn, too. It's a determination from their perspective of how risky you are as a borrower. A credit report provides a picture of how well you handled your debt and obligations. It's a record of where you work, where you live, how you pay your debts, whether you have judgments or liens (now *there's* a grown-up word, meaning the right to of a company to keep possession of your property until you have paid your debt) against you, and any bankruptcies you may have filed in the last ten years.

What hurts your credit report and score?
- Missed payments.
- Large debt loads.
- Collections accounts.
- Having no credit history at all.

How do you improve your score?

- Build savings first, then use credit.
- Try to only use credit cards when you can pay in full each month.
- Make payments on time month after month.
- Use savings, not credit cards, for emergencies like losing a job, fixing a broken vehicle, or paying medical bills.

WHERE TO GET YOUR CREDIT REPORT

Remember those Free Credit Report commercials? When their ads were everywhere, I could start playing one and the audience would sing the whole song from memory.

When something has recognition to the point that everyone is familiar with it, you can bet it's a business that's making money. Even a small amount of advertising can be really expensive, yet the Free Credit Report people do massive amounts of advertising.

Seriously, how could a company that offers free credit reports actually make money?

Simple. By not offering free credit reports. If you watch one of their commercials, at the very end you'll see a little text pop up that says, "Offer only applies with enrollment in Triple Advantage."[50]

Hmm.

It's always adorable when television commercials try to do the equivalent of fine print at the bottom of a contract explaining the "catch." They are legally bound to include it, but they can't plant it somewhere in a long page of text, or make the font really tiny. They have to say it out loud. So they think, "We'll just say it faster and in a deeper voice! No one will notice!"

It turns out that to get a free credit report from FreeCreditReport.com, you must enroll in a program called Triple Advantage, which costs $14.95. I guess "$15CreditReport.com" wasn't as catchy.

Good news. The federal government-endorsed web site at www.annualcreditreport.com gives you one free credit report per year from each of the three main reporting agencies (TransUnion, Equifax, and Experian).

I recommend you pull the government one and get a sense of what your credit looks like. Or you can check out the actually free service at www.creditkarma.com, which will run your credit and give you a credit score. It does for credit scores what www.mint.com does for budgeting.

LET'S RECAP: HOW YOU'LL WIN BY OUTSMARTING CREDIT CARDS

The simple formula for how to win with credit is that when you do make a purchase with a card, immediately pay it off. Don't carry your balance into another month. Pay it off right away.

Keep in mind that good credit consists primarily of two things: a history of on-time payments, and a history of carrying low balances from month to month.

If you follow this formula, then it is fine to use a credit card to establish good credit, or to acquire some of the incentives offered by your credit card provider. But if you can't afford to pay for it in cash, then you can't afford to pay for it.

My recommendation is this: if you do not fully understand how credit cards work, do not get one.

Most people struggle to establish good credit, either because they have out-of-control spending habits, or because credit cards themselves are full of pitfalls, ensuring that more people end up with bad credit, and thus, owe more money.

There is a phrase that credit cards companies use behind closed doors to describe people who do not make minimum payments, but rather pay in full. These people don't end up owing interest, because they do not get caught by the tricks that credit cards provide. Know what that phrase is?

"Deadbeats."[51]

That paints a picture, doesn't it? Let's you know how the companies see people who use the service to their own advantage, but don't wind up paying interest charges.

I don't say this a lot, but *be a deadbeat*. When it comes to a credit card, do not let them win. Be careful with that card, use it carefully, avoid the risks, and you'll avoid paying a lot extra.

Now what are some ways you can do this?

First off, a debit card is a much safer alternative to a credit card because it takes money out of your account that you already have. You can overdraw by a little, but you can't overspend by a lot. You can also look at getting a charge card that automatically withdraws the full amount borrowed every month from your bank account. This creates a debit card system for you, while you get the bonuses of using credit. These cards make it so you aren't allowed to make minimum payments.

The best suggestion I can give you, though, is to look for a low-limit credit card, so you won't be able to borrow more than you can pay back.

But here's a caveat. If you handle your credit card well, you may get a letter in the mail saying, "Congratulations, you have done such a good job with your credit card, we have raised your limit to . . . (some higher amount)."

This happens to a lot of people. It sounds great, but it's the opposite of good news. You've managed your credit because you know your limit and how much you can pay back quickly, without incurring interest. Raising the limit means a higher risk that you won't be able to pay back what you're now able to spend.

So don't take that letter as good news. Write them or call them back and say, "No, thank you; I want my credit card at a low limit, because I am trying to be safe." Don't tell them you're trying to be a deadbeat. That's our joke.

BONUS SECTION: An Extremely Short History of Credit Cards

While borrowing has been around forever, credit cards are a relatively new invention. Back in the 1800s, merchants and financial intermediaries began providing credit for the purchase of agricultural and durable goods. The practice soon spread to other industries: hotels and department stores gave their most valued customers paper cards mainly used at one location. Some local merchants would even accept a competitors' card.

Building off the success of a popular restaurant diner's card at the time, Bank of America introduced the first general-purpose credit card in the late 1950s.

The bank then created a separate credit card operation in the mid-1970s that eventually became VISA (Visa International Service Association). A network of rival cards beginning in 1966 eventually became the association we know as MasterCard.[52]

The credit card industry has always courted controversy over high fees and interest rates, often hidden in complex credit agreements. In the 1970s and 1980s, politicians allowed a process of "deregulation" of the industry.[53] Many lending practices became acceptable and legal that led consumers deeper into debt, resulting in a cascade of mass defaults (walking away from unpaid loans) that eventually played a role in the collapse of the American economy in 2008. In 2010, President Obama signed the Dodd-Frank Wall Street Reform and Consumer Protection Act into law. The bill had been lobbied in Congress for decades, and it curbed some of the most controversial credit card practices like ballooning interest rates, unseemly penalties, and relentless marketing to college students.

It changed things, but not as much as we'd hoped.

Today the average household carries credit card debt of just under $15,000, with many using cards that still carry last year's holiday debt to pay for this year's season. There are 181 million cardholders, with the typical cardholder having five cards in their name. That's over 900 million credit cards in service.

That gives you some sense of it. I bring it back to us, and to everyday life, because we can see the most change by changing our behavior around, and values toward, the ability to borrow.

ACTION PLAN: FOUR STEPS TO DEFEAT YOUR DEBT

1. Pick a Payoff Strategy

Your goal is to pay off your loans, not live off them. There are two main philosophies around paying off your debt.

Debt Snowball: you pick the smallest debt you have first, and pay it off because this will create a sense of accomplishment and momentum to pay off your next smallest debt.

Debt Avalanche: pay off your debt with the highest interest first.

Neither one is better than the other, but one of these is better for you. Pick the one that suits your personality more.

Bonus Tip: Play the Debt Game

A friend of mine pays off her debt by treating it like it's a game. Each month, she'll take her current student loan debt, and make a payment that makes the next month's debt total a round number. Rather than just make flat payments, she looks at it like she's trying to get the highest score.

Remember, making minimum payments is a strategy that benefits those you owe, not you. Minimum payments, maximum cost. The bigger the payment the closer you are to being debt-free. Maximum payments, minimum cost.

2. Get a Spending Tracker

Every person in the world needs a budget, rich and poor, in debt or not. But when you're in debt, you need a budget more than ever. There are a couple great options available:

Mint: (www.mint.com) Mint is completely free, secure, and created by the people who make Quicken. You link all debit and credit cards to your Mint account, and every purchase you make on them will be recorded and categorized. (You will need to do some correcting of its auto-categorization, but not much.) Do this for one month, and then make sure everything is categorized correctly. Now you have totals on how much you spend in each category. Do these numbers work for you? Are there any you need to cut back on? These totals, after a few small and realistic adjustments, become totals for your monthly spending plan for next month.

Choose one or two categories tops to cut back on for the next month, and identify the amount of money you're willing to spend in those categories. Now see how you do. This is where you'll learn about yourself, because you either change your behavior or you change your budget to rationalize your behavior.

YouNeedABudget: (www.youneedabudget.com) Even though at the time of this writing YNAB costs money (but offers a free trial), many people prefer YNAB to Mint because you have to literally track every expense you make. This makes you way more conscious of your spending, but also requires a lot more effort than Mint. People who use YNAB love it, and rave about the community and free resources and videos you'll get access to when you join (even in trial).

Bonus Tip: An App for Debt Repayment Tracking

The **Pay Off Debt** App (www.thedebtmyth.com) doesn't track your overall spending, but it tracks your progress in paying back your loans. It's an investment in a plan that's going to save you a lot more than that.

3. Have an Emergency Fund

Surprisingly, the first step in getting out of debt is not paying it down, it's saving up. An emergency fund is your cushion should something unexpected happen that—if you didn't have the fund—would force you to put more debt on your credit card.

An emergency fund protects you from increasing your debt.

How much should you keep in your emergency fund? There are two ways to answer that. First you might ask yourself, "How much did my last emergency cost?" Now save to that amount.

The second is to go with the generally accepted rules of thumb around emergency funds: you should save up at least one month of living expenses. After one month of budgeting, you'll know what your monthly cost of living is. In your first few months of defeating your debt, you can utilize what we call a Scrape Season, which is a total spending shut down. Reduce extraneous costs in any way you can. Don't go into stores. Don't go out to eat. Don't have fun. Find out how much you absolutely have to have to get through a month, and embrace how much life sucks while you're doing that.

Because here's the great news: it sucks for a reason, and only for a little while. Once you have saved up your target number, you can go back to spending as normal. Or, if you like the feeling of money in the bank, you can save up more—maybe three months' worth of living expenses. It's an incredibly powerful thing to have three to six months of living expenses in your bank account.

4. Identify a Strong Incentive

This is the most important thing you can do, and you're doing this one for your future self. You should be hungry for the day you'll get out of debt, because the relief you will feel and the freedom and opportunity that will come with it are better than the pleasure ANY purchase will bring you.

How do you act on behalf of your future (debt-free) self? By visualizing what it will be like to make your last payment. Where will you be? Will you throw a massive party? I hope so! Will you experience life without the stress of having this debt hanging over you? You will, and you will love it. So visualize it.

I know this is challenging. But it's also so important.

Talk to yourself as a person who is paying off her or his debt. Arm yourself with these 'take a stand' statements:[54]

- *I am the kind of person who only spends money I already have.*
- *My family deserves a debt-free life.*
- *I no longer borrow money to pay for things. I rely on hard work and resourcefulness instead.*
- *I will be debt-free by [date] or sooner. (Insert the date you've calculated, maybe using the Pay Off Debt app.)*
- *I prepare for emergencies and save until I have the money for the things I want and need.*

- *I am/will be debt free because* _____
  _____. *(Fill in your reason)*
- *I live a debt-free life.*
- *(Or create your own positive finance-related phrase.)*

Pick one and make it the wallpaper on your phone, or put it where you'll see it every day. Say it yourself whenever you are tempted to violate your get-out-of-debt plan.

Bonus Tip: Get a buddy who you can check in with, judgment-free, about how well you're doing. All goals need accountability and support.

You *can* do this. Your 'Finally-Debt-Free' party awaits.

CHAPTER 5:

MAKING MONEY

"Our work is to discover our work and then with all our heart to give ourselves to it."

— Buddha

GRANDMANOMICS

Even though she stood only 4'9", my grandma was the most powerful woman I've ever met. She was from South Africa, and her English accent made her resemble a late-era Audrey Hepburn. She spoke English, Swahili, Xhosa, and Zulu.

Because we lived on different continents, I can remember every one of my gran's visits. She would teach me to play card games, the object being less about winning and more about creatively and memorably heckling each other.

I also remember she would talk to anyone and everyone she encountered. It was so embarrassing. Every time you looked away, she would march off towards the nearest group of people. By the time you turned back, she'd be holding both of the hands of some poor, cornered stranger, staring up into their eyes, and asking them personal questions.

"Are you happy in your life?"

"How much money do you make?"

Her favorite question: "Do you have any discounts for an old woman?"

She got a lot of discounts.

As a child, I thought this was supremely embarrassing, but the truth is people loved her. As I got older I stopped worrying about whether she would talk to every single person in line (she would), because I realized my gran was demonstrating a secret of making money: get noticed and get feedback.

These two steps will help you practice putting yourself out there.

Practice is key. When comedians test out new material on an audience, they go to events called open mics. There, they get a chance to try out ideas. If the audience laughs, the idea becomes a joke. If nobody laughs, it remains just an idea. To this day, I don't trust that an idea is a joke until I've tested it on an audience. It's not as scary as it sounds. The audience in the room is usually pretty kind. Your toughest audience is you.

So getting noticed is a way of getting feedback.

When you see the people around you as holding opportunities for you, or at least consider that they're able to give you feedback you can learn from, like the audience at an open mic, they become less threatening. They can help you. Do the work of approaching people with your ideas, and choose not to doubt yourself. Make them tell you your idea is a bad one. They certainly will, and then you can delete it from your process, freeing you up to try something new the next time. This is all assuming you'll be bad. You might be great. But if you never audition for something, whatever your reason is for not doing it, you can be sure you are never going to see that idea pay off for you.

Success is not just about being good at what you do. It's about creating your own opportunities. You never know when you might catch the attention of someone with the power to make your dream a reality.

In the first year of my program, I toured schools with a band. Even though they were a few years out of college, these musicians had had some pretty serious success. When I asked them how they make a living as performers, they all said the same thing.

"Gigonomics."

They'd play every gig they could play. Success is a numbers game. You take every gig, even the decidedly non-rock'n'roll ones, like the Sunday BBQ church picnics, because you never know who will be in the audience. You never know who might come up to you after the show and offer you your next gig or opportunity.

And if you're not musically inclined, then practice Grandmanomics. Practice starting conversations with lots of people, and learn how to grow from the feedback you get.

HOW TO ACTUALLY "DO WHAT YOU LOVE"

Most everyone tells you to "find your passion," but few tell you how. Let's break down the world of work into paths to happiness and success, and the many ways to get there. In this chapter we're going to talk about things like getting the right schooling, how to plan out your career, and how you can make both a living and a difference simultaneously.

If you find yourself feeling more confused than encouraged by the advice to "find your passion," you're not alone. I've felt so, so lost throughout my education and attempts at a career after college. I just had no real sense of direction. It's tough. And most people feel this way at some point.

If you have yet to identify the kind of work that would fulfill you, then your current work is to be curious. Your job is try out all kinds of different jobs. And not just the obviously fun ones like being an athlete or a performer. There are tons of people who don't love what they do during the workweek, but love what it affords them the ability to do with the rest of their time.

If you're looking for guidance based on your current skills or even simply things you like to do, you can find out which careers they line up with by using the Bureau of Labor Statistics career exploration website: http://www.bls.gov/k12/content/students/careers/career-exploration.htm.

And if you do have a creative vision for your life, one that includes a lot of challenges ahead and lessons to be learned, then pursuing it means working harder over the short term than most people ever would so over the long term we are able to live like most people never could. That's what the career search is. You'll find lots of pleasant-enough stopping points along the way, but if you keep searching, you'll eventually find work you love.

Let's talk about four categories that totally qualify as finding your passion.

1) Get paid to do work you love

Find something you love to do, and then figure out how to make a living at it. The reality is that passion can live in all sorts of places. And while finding your passion is an elusive pursuit, there is only one real formula: try things. Try things and see how they fit. Try jobs and find out what you like, and just as importantly, what you don't like.

The best way to do this in school is to seek out an internship at a local company. You should talk to your guidance/career counselors, or your parents, or a friend's parents who you think are awesome. If you're no longer a student, invite a person out for coffee whose career and profession interest you. Bring a bunch of questions and just chat. People love to tell their story. Go to listen, and you will learn in one conversation what would have taken you ten years to figure out on your own.

Try as many things as possible, until you fall in love with something. Take a class. Take a risk. Sign up for something you're not sure you're good at. Talk to people who do what you love and ask for their advice. Say "yes" to an internship or low-paying job that seems intriguing. (You'll either save yourself time by discovering you don't like that work, or you'll solve the problem by discovering you really like it AND start building a network then and there!)

Since 2009, I've had the good fortune of knowing what I want to spend the rest of my life doing. It's been really fulfilling. It has also brought me some of the toughest experiences I've ever had. There have even been times when I wished I didn't know what my direction was, and I wished I could go back to pretending that any job that pays the bills would be enough for me.

This is because, in the process of pursuing your passion, you'll discover it's not just about doing what you're good at. It isn't just about capitalizing on your strengths, it's also identifying your weaknesses—the ones that can't be ignored—and then knuckling down and either transforming them into strengths or succeeding enough financially to get other people to do those parts for you.

And that's challenging, exhausting, humbling, and eventually, incredible. The pursuit of our passion, of the best version of ourselves, is one of the most difficult pursuits for this very reason.

2) Get paid to afford what makes you happy

In other words, find something that pays you to do what you love in your non-work hours. What do you love to do? Play music? Travel? Eat incredible meals? Write code? Help people in need?

Pick something, and then look for tasks you can do (not necessarily connected to those things) that will provide you with the money you need to do them for the rest of your life. Ideally, it'll be something that doesn't consume all of your time and energy in the process. In other words, rather than work your passion, work to finance your passion.

Think about "make vs. need." We spend too much time asking ourselves how much we want to make when we could be asking a better question: how much money do I need to meet my expenses? That's a quantifiable number.

A good, round number for the living expenses of young adults who don't have student loans but have their own apartments (and roommates) and cars is about $30,000-$40,000 a year. If you find a job that pays you that amount, you can pursue the thing you love in all the rest of your time, for as many years as you want.

3) Get paid to do something you're good at

Find out how to enjoy the work itself, either by finding something you're good at, or by developing your ability to feel joy and gratitude.

There is great joy to be found in excelling at something. Hard work is highly rewarding when you see the progress you're making and the impact it's having on its intended audience. Every time you challenge yourself in your work, you grow. And every time you look back on yourself earlier in your work, when you thought you were the best you'd ever be, you see how much better you are now. That's a life of growth and evolution—very fulfilling stuff!

Billionaire Mark Cuban said:

When you work hard at something you become good at it. When you become good at doing something, you will enjoy it more. When you enjoy doing something, there is a very good chance you will become passionate or more passionate about it. When you are good at something, you're passionate and you work even harder to excel and be the best at it, good things happen. Don't follow your passions, follow your effort.[55]

While you can't always choose what you do, you can always choose how you do it. Are you grateful? Are you peacekeeping? Are you invested in the success of others? Are you able to face yourself and be proud of who you are? You can be a happy millionaire, or you can be a miserable one. You can also work an unglamorous job and choose to be excited every single day. Which kind of person would you rather be around? Choose to be that one. What you do doesn't have to define you, but you do. In fact, it's up to you to define yourself, for yourself. Because if you don't, then your work, the people around you, or your life circumstances will.

It's not just about what you do, it's about how you do it. Happiness is an important consideration when thinking about money. So is fulfillment.

A good friend of mine works in the nonprofit world, while his sister works in the corporate world. They've each made different choices based on their interests, and it won't surprise you to know his sister makes a lot more money than he does. He told me, "You know, it's hard. Whenever I see her lifestyle and all the money she has, I find myself thinking, 'I wish I had your paycheck.' But then I realize that if I were getting her paychecks, that would mean I'd have her job. And I definitely wouldn't want that."

Most of us struggle with the fantasy that having a lot of money would fix our problems. So we work hard to get paid well. Yet sometimes the work meant to bring us that happiness makes us miserable instead. Spending the most energetic hours of your day doing something that makes you miserable can be the quickest route to becoming a lifelong, high-spending consumer.

Next time you think, "I wish had their paycheck," remember no amount of money will feel worth it if you don't want to spend your life doing that job. Good news: there are other kinds of paychecks and other kinds of satisfaction. Taking a risk increases your confidence, just like doing a job increases your money. Achieving something increases your self-worth. Helping others increases your happiness.

And when managing your finances comes into it, as in everything else, there's a relationship between our fulfillment in our work and our ability to control our money habits We'll bring that idea home soon.

4) Get paid to do the wrong thing while you search for the right thing

I'm not talking about a back-up plan. I'm talking about a start-up plan.

Whatever dream you have for your life takes more than just desire. It takes a plan—a plan that involves hard work, kindness to others, and confidence. If I wanted to use my talents to make the world better (and I did), I had to understand how the world worked before I could get the world to work for me.

People used to tell me that it seemed like I had a plan. Personally, I didn't feel like I had one. Maybe they saw something in me I didn't see in myself. Or maybe they recognized what I now recognize, which is that saving money and learning every skill I could in order to be my best self functions the same way a plan does. You don't have to know where you're going, as long as you're willing to build and refine healthy habits. Now I know this process is essentially laying the foundation to build your life on. You won't know it at the time, but when your big idea arrives, you'll discover you're all set to pursue it.

You can look at the work you're doing now as an opportunity to save the money and build the skills you'll need for your dream job. It's not easy to enjoy working at a job you don't really like. You can let that frustration motivate you to find joy by spending more money, buying expensive clothes, going on expensive trips, or eating and drinking a lot more. Or you can let that frustration motivate you to work toward something better.

When someone gives you a hard time about your new, thrifty money habits, and they will, feel free to mess with their heads. Tell them, "I've got a plan."

The number of overnight successes in the world is incredibly small. Yet the number of people who reached success on a level they never thought possible through hard work, building relationships, and perseverance is massive. Your start-up plan is all about how to invest in yourself.

How about an example?

A NEW HOLLYWOOD LEGEND

In 1996, a recently graduated English Literature major named Chris conceived of an idea for a film. The film would be about a blocked writer who starts following people out of boredom, only to eventually realize he is being followed himself. He ends up being slowly drawn into a decidedly un-boring world of danger and deception by a mysterious woman and a charismatic thief.

Chris shot the film over the course of a year while still working his full-time job. He cast his friends and his girlfriend as the leads. They shot only on Saturdays, on film, with no crew to help them. The result was *Following*, a remarkably polished and atmospheric black-and-white film that had intricate dialogue, strong acting, and a complex plot. It cost Chris $6,000, and is still one of the cheapest films ever made.

Following got him the funding for his second film, *Memento*, the film which got him officially discovered and kicked off a storied directing career that includes *Batman Begins*, *The Dark Knight*, and *Inception*. Chris is Christopher Nolan.

This isn't just a success story; this is a financial template for success.

In an industry where many people feel obligated to raise and spend millions of dollars on a film for it to stand out, Chris actually found a way to hack the Hollywood film machine. He treated his first film like it was merely the prelude to his second film. He acted less like he was making a movie and more like he was starting a business. Chris's own job supplied most of his start-up money (the job acted as what many entrepreneurs call a "base," paying your living while you work nights and weekends). He also managed to pay any unexpected overhead that arose from shooting and marketing the film out of his salary. No debt.

Chris kept his costs low by filling the main roles with his friends, as well as his fiancée. Every scene was rehearsed for weeks so they could shoot it in only one or two takes, which saved on the cost of film. He not only made a good film, but he did so in such a way that it was incredibly difficult for him to go into debt on it.

When you start a small business, you quickly realize that your own living expenses are part of the overall budget of the business. If the average person needs a rough minimum of $30,000 a year to live on their own, to maintain a car, pay for their food, etc., then those expenses get added in to what the business needs to provide. Holding down an extra job at the start is a useful way of paying those costs without putting undue pressure on your developing business—pressures that could otherwise compromise your project and your vision for doing it the right way.

PATHWAYS TO EARNING

In his book *Outliers,* author Malcolm Gladwell identifies three qualities that work must have to be considered satisfying, fulfilling work: autonomy, complexity, and a connection between effort and reward.[56]

What types of careers are out there to supply these qualities?

That's the beautiful thing about the future—you can be as creative as you want with this question. You can try lots of things and figure it out. Below are two pathways and two different kinds of work.

PATHWAY 1: LEARN FIRST

There are a lot of jobs that require you to have a college degree. As I mentioned earlier, this doesn't have to be a four-year degree. "College" can be seen as a catchall category for any post-secondary education: certification, associate's degree, bachelor's degree, technical training, apprenticeship, etc.

The four-year-college-for-every-student argument doesn't serve every student equally. But it also doesn't mean you don't need any college. You could skip all post-high school education and earn money sooner by working at a grocery store or gas station. But you'll likely earn less, maybe for the rest of your life, because you won't qualify for better-paying jobs.

In many fields, employment opportunities that don't require a four-year degree are growing faster than those that do.[57] In 'The Associate's Degree Payoff,' www.economicmodeling.com posted this data about non-college jobs that pay well:

Highest Paying Jobs for Associate's Degrees[58]

Career	Hourly	Annual
Radiation Therapists	$37.36	$77,709
Dental Hygienists	$34.77	$72,322
Nuclear Medicine Technologists	$33.96	$70,637
Nuclear Technicians	$32.85	$68,328
Diagnostic Medical Sonographers	$31.83	$66,206
Aerospace Engineering and Operations Technicians	$29.48	$61,318
Engineering Technicians, Except Drafters, All Other	$28.54	$59,363
Respiratory Therapists	$27.04	$56,243

These jobs require certification or a two-year degree, and that could be a lot more cost-effective for you than a four-year college degree.

PATHWAY 2: EARN FIRST

There are other jobs where you can start work immediately because they tend to require one specific skill. I worked in data entry, and the only skill I needed was the ability to type fast. It was a good job, but it also bored me to tears.

Which is why it's so important to ask more than "How much does it pay?" You need to know if the work you're looking at will be satisfying and safe, and what other costs might be associated with it. Let's consider a few examples.

Automotive: Do I have to provide my own tools? If so, what would they cost?

Construction: Can I work all four seasons of the year? If not, how will I finance my expenses during the seasons when work is scarce? If I get injured on the weekend and I can't work till I recover, what will I do for money in the meantime?

Creative Careers: What are the upfront costs of becoming a filmmaker, a writer, a comedian, or an actor?

At the end of your chosen pathway lies your work. You could work for an employer, be an employer, or be your own employer. Being your own boss (also called being an entrepreneur) can look very different depending on the work you do. You could start a construction firm, retail store, professional office, product manufacture/sales, etc. There are a variety of different legal statuses for businesses, from independent freelancer to sole-proprietorship, limited liability, S-corporation, partnership, etc. All are similar in the way they impact your financial life, but freelancing, which is the simplest and most common level of self-employment or side-employment, tends to have less start-up cost.

PATHWAY 3: FREELANCE

You can freelance after going to school, as a creative writer, accountant, child-care professional, business-consulting etc., or you can freelance before going to school, as a graphic designer, day care provider, dog walker, basic home repair, basic landscaper, etc.

Being a freelancer is pretty interesting. You get to set your own schedule. You also pay for that privilege through higher tax rates and paying for your own healthcare premiums.

For instance, full-time employees who make less than $35,350 pay 7.5% of their income in taxes, and their employer pays the other 7.5%. Freelancers and entrepreneurs pay the whole 15% themselves. And any income you earn above the tax bracket of $35,350 is taxed at a higher, corresponding rate.

Here is an example of income tax brackets:

Mar-ginal Tax Rate	Single	Married Filing Jointly or Qualified Widow(er)	Married Filing Separately	Head of Household
10%	$0 to $8,700	$0 to $17,400	$0 to $8,700	$0 to $12,400
15%	$8,700 to $35,350	$17,400 to $70,700	$8,700 to $35,350	$12,400 to $47,350
25%	$35,350 to $85,650	$70,700 to $142,700	$35,350 to $71,350	$47,350 to $122,300
28%	$85,650 to $178,650	$142,700 to $217,450	$71,350 to $108,725	$122,300 to $198,050
33%	$178,650 to $388,350	$217,450 to $388,350	$108,725 to $194,175	$198,050 to $388,350
35%	$388,350+	$388,350+	$194,175	$388,350+

As a freelancer, you should get a contract for work you agree to do. I still have this business card from a guy I worked with as a freelancer. He offered to pay me to write up his website copy for his business. I took tons of notes, went through all his resources and files, and turned them into five or six strong, carefully crafted pages of information. I sent him an invoice for my fifteen hours of work, and never heard from him again. Because we had a handshake agreement, I had no way to advocate for myself. I didn't get paid a dime. And after I delivered the work, all he had to do is just never respond to my emails. I learned a cold, hard lesson that day: without a contract, you might get conned into working for free.

An interesting opportunity is that you can name your own price. As a freelancer, you can set the value on your work. You might even name a price higher than you might think you're worth. This takes some confidence to do (and some research on your industry, so you don't price yourself out of jobs), but it allows you to raise your pay much faster than might happen if you went to your full-time boss and asked for a raise.

PATHWAY 4: RUN YOUR OWN BUSINESS

Ultimately, starting a business can be a very risky, very costly, very challenging, and very exciting undertaking.

People will often quote the statistic, "90% of businesses fail in the first two years." Don't let them discourage you, because they're wrong. The correct statistic is that 33% of businesses fail in their first four years.[59]

So that's good news.

And more good news: the entrepreneur's business model can actually be more financially stable than being a full-time employee at any one company. I'll explain:

When you are self-employed (own your own business), you work for whoever pays you. Instead of one boss paying you, you may have a number of bosses paying you. If you lose one of those bosses, the effect is far less catastrophic on you than if all of your money were coming in from that one place.

When you work for clients, you go from having one employer to having many employers. This means when you work for yourself there is no set limit to how much you can earn. There is no minimum you can earn either.

Here are some of the basic costs of having your own business:

Licensing: You may want to file with your state as an LLC (limited liability company), which is less complicated than a corporation, but more involved than sole proprietorship, or fully incorporate, typically for an annual fee. The fees vary by state.

Equipment: Any equipment you need, from a computer to a printer to server space to a truck, becomes your cost.

Advertising: One of the challenges I initially fell into with my business was this idea that the world would somehow know I was now available and would come looking for me. Nope. If you struggle with marketing and advertising, you must accept that you are now the marketing department of your business. Those costs are on you, and also the challenge of learning how to do those functions well. Either that, or you have to earn enough to pay someone to do it for you.

No matter what service you're hoping to provide, when you make that your business you must develop the skills to promote and sell your service.

Yourself: An interesting thought—as a person with income and expenses, you are a business already. The practice of starting your own business simply makes it more concrete. This also means your own lifestyle expenses become part of the overall expenses of your business.

Because starting a business can cost money, if this is what you want to do, it's a great idea to start budgeting your personal expenses now. These habits will directly influence your ability to make it through the first few (and likely leanest) years of your new business. It's also a great time to start building the skill of saving money— savings that will become your start-up fund.

THE HAPPINESS SALARY

What level of salary will make you happy? As reported in *TIME Magazine* in September 2010, a study from Princeton University's Woodrow Wilson School found that money actually can buy happiness, up to about $75,000 a year.[60]

The study was conducted by economist Angus Deaton and psychologist Daniel Kahneman (a Nobel Prize winner in Economics). The researchers analyzed the responses of 450,000 Americans polled by the Gallup and Healthways organizations in 2008 and 2009.

So, why $75,000?

What they found was that the further people's annual income fell below $75,000, the unhappier they felt. And that no matter how much more than $75,000 people made, they didn't report any greater degree of happiness.

"The study doesn't say why $75,000 is the benchmark," explained Deaton in the *TIME* article. "But it does seem to me a plausible number at which people would think money is not an issue."

So, while being financially successful can lead you to feel that your life is working out as a whole, you can still be grumpy in the morning and cranky in traffic.

Making less than this amount does not directly cause sadness, but it can lead to life's problems feeling more overwhelming. There's simply less cushion.

At $75,000, that effect disappears. At that level of earning, according to the research, individual temperament and life circumstances have a greater effect on happiness than money.

SUDDEN WEALTH SYNDROME

In 2011 researchers conducted a teen survey on behalf of the financial institution Charles Schwab. In the report, called "Teens and Money," the kids surveyed all anticipated a future career with an average income of $150,000 per year.[61] And they're not the only ones who apparently think that way. Lots of us have big dreams. But the reality is, not very many people make that much money. In fact, 95% of Americans do not earn $150,000 per year.[62]

Let me be clear. These teens aren't dumb. Many of them have not handled their own expenses before, so it's fine if their estimates are a little off the mark. Besides, it's a very relatable thing to wish for. Wouldn't it be great to make so much money you don't have to be careful with it any longer? With massive amounts of money coming in, who needs to think about budgeting? Or face not having enough to pay your bills? Or going into debt? We could essentially "out-earn" our financial problems.

But that's missing the real opportunity for financial freedom your income offers you. Suppose we *are* earning that $150,000 every year. We can spend it on a lot of stuff. Maybe we spend as much as $140,000 a year. That's OK, because we're saving $10,000 a year, even though we're spending 93% of our income.

Now, what about if we earn $30,000 per year and our expenses are $20,000? We're saving the same $10,000, but we're only spending 67% of our income in the process. This is a much more impressive margin. And you are practicing a financial skill that'll come in handy should you lose your income for a period of time. You're less financially fragile.

Most people's expenses increase to the level of their earning, even if they make a great deal of money. It's called induced consumption, or more memorably, sudden wealth syndrome. That's what's so tough—spending impulsively and for pleasure is an easy habit to form. We just stop thinking about it, and we spend it. When we don't acknowledge this common trap, and instead fall into induced consumption, earning a lot can still end up feeling like not enough. Becoming aware of our habits is the first step, and the next is not to change our behavior, but our thinking.

If you achieve your wealth rather than being born into it, then wealth is a direction rather than a destination. You are either headed toward it, or you are headed away from it, but you're always in motion. So the secret to becoming and remaining successful is to change your thinking.

A man named Mr. Allan is a great example of the way we could be thinking about our money. "The Millionaire Next Door" explains the way the multi-millionaire thinks about his money:

Mr. Allan, as well as those people whom he has backed financially, has never felt that his purpose in life was to look wealthy. According to Mr. Allan, 'That's why I'm financially independent. If your goal is to become financially secure, you'll likely attain it . . . But if your motive is to make money to spend money on the good life, . . . you're never gonna make it.' Allan stated numerous times: 'Money should never change one's values. Making money is only a report card. It's a way to tell how you're doing.'[63]

THE STOCK MARKET IN SIMPLE TERMS

What often distinguishes the wealthy mind from the non-wealthy mind is being willing to ask questions about what we don't know, and no area inspires more confusion or mystery than the world of investing.

An investment, simply put, is when you put money into a financial product (like a Certificate of Deposit, a stock, a bond, or a mutual fund) in the hopes that over time it will increase in value and earn you interest.

In this situation, you are using your money to make you more money. Your money is working for you, while you are working, or napping, or watching TV, or whatever. This is called passive income.

When it goes well, investing creates passive income. Of course, there are no guarantees that your financial product might not lose its value, so you couldn't get the money back that you originally put in. Risk is a key component of investing, and it should never be ignored.

I'm going to explain how this stuff works, but you should always seek out the advice of a qualified financial adviser. Remember, you absolutely must ask them about their qualifications and make sure they are a fiduciary.

A broker is an individual or company qualified to purchase these investments for you or you can do it at your financial institution.

A full-service broker: Carries out "buy" and "sell" orders for clients, provides expertise and advice, in exchange for a commission.

A discount broker: Carries out "buy" and "sell" orders at a reduced commission, since the broker provides no investment advice. Thanks to discount brokers, nearly anybody can afford to invest in the market. But you have to do your own research.

An online broker: Facilitates access to markets online, but you do the work. Examples: E*Trade, Scottrade, Ameritrade, ShareBuilder, and the like.

A Bond: When you buy a bond, you make a loan to a company or a government. They pay you interest over the life of the bond, until "maturity" (when the bond has reached the end of an agreed bond cycle), at which point, they pay you back the original amount. So if I buy a three-year maturity bond from CareBearsCorp for $1,000 at 5%, they will pay me 5% of $1000 ($50) every month for three years, plus they'll pay me back my $1,000. So I walk away with $1,800.[64]

Since the investor receives regular interest payments from the bond issuer until the bond matures, this means that a bond actually pays interest-only over the duration (or term) of the bond.

In the US, you can buy bonds directly from the government through TreasuryDirect at http://www.treasurydirect.gov.

A Certificate Of Deposit (CD): This is a financial product wherein you invest a certain amount of money and promise not to use any of it for a period of time. At the end of the term, you'll get your money back plus a higher level of interest earned on that sum of money. Of course you have to be sure you won't need the money for the length of the term (could be a year or several years), because taking it out early will result in penalties. If you can let it stay in the CD, it's a safe and predictable way to get you a higher interest rate on your money.

A Stock: Stock is a share in a business. When you buy a share, you become a part owner of the business, meaning that you receive a percentage of the company's profits, based on how big a chunk of the business you now own (one share is usually a very small piece, but people can often buy hundreds or thousands of shares in a company). Stocks can be volatile: they fluctuate on a daily basis. High return. High risk. You lose money when a stock decreases in value. You make money when the stock goes up.

A Mutual Fund: A mutual fund is a financial product composed of stocks and shares from many companies. It's an example of diversifying—by spreading out your investment over multiple companies' stocks included in the mutual fund, you end up spreading out your risk. You can get a mutual fund that is actively managed by a professional adviser, or you may want to consider an index fund, which mirrors the distribution of the stock market as a whole.

To learn more about investments and the stock market, check out The Stock Market Game www.stockmarketgame.com, a program of the Securities Industry and Financial Markets Association (SIFMA) Foundation.

An Asset (Real Estate/A Business): By purchasing a house you are operating on the belief that home values will go up over time. This is often the case, although the 2008 burst in the housing bubble deeply rattled this notion. It's important to know that a house is not really a profitable investment if you're only going to own it for a short amount of time.

When I was in college, I knew a student who bought property during college and all his friends lived in it and paid him rent. He sold it when they graduated, and ended up paying less than he would have if he'd rented.

A LITTLE BIT ON COMPOUND INTEREST

Albert Einstein called compound interest the greatest mathematical discovery of all time, saying, "Those who understand compound interest are destined to collect it. Those who don't are doomed to pay it."

Simply put, collecting compound interest means collecting interest *on* your interest. If you invest an amount of money at a fixed interest, and you take the interest earned on your money out of the account at the end of every year, your money will grow at the same rate, year after year. But if you leave the money in, and you leave the interest earnings in, then the rate of growth will increase due to compound interest.

With compound interest, the amount of money you collect in interest goes up every year, because now you're collecting interest on the original principal plus the interest you earned from the past year. The longer the money is invested, the larger the principal grows. Interest on your interest = compound interest.

Here's how it would make a difference right away. Start with $1,000.

Year	Principal	Rate	Interest
1	$1,000.00	2.93%	$29.30
2	$1,029.30	2.93%	$30.16
3	$1,059.46	2.93%	$31.04
4	$1,090.50	2.93%	$31.95
5	$1,122.45	2.93%	$32.89

And this is how it works over a long period of time. The differences are striking.

Time	Simple	Compound
Year 1	$1,100	$1,100
Year 5	$1,500	$1,610
Year 10	$2,000	$2,593
Year 20	$3,000	$6,727

Time	Simple	Compound
Year 30	$4,000	$17,449
Year 40	$5,000	$45,259
Year 50	$6,000	$117,390

I'm explaining this concept in years to keep it simple, but you should know that compound interest is calculated every day, which makes for an even better investment return because you don't have to wait till the end of the year to get the benefit.

THE RULE OF 72

In a recent college poll, over 80% of the students surveyed did not know what the Rule of 72 was.[65] You're about to join the other twenty percent.

The Rule of 72 states: divide your interest rate by 72 to get a rough estimate of how many years it will take for your invested money to double. (This is a ballpark formula, not an exact mathematical formula.)

72 / Your Interest Rate = Years Till Your $ Doubles

When asked, 80% of the students didn't know what this was. Yet in the same poll, over 80% of the students surveyed knew how long Kim Kardashian was married to Kris Humphries: 72 days.

So how can we remember that? Let's call it the Kardashian Rule. Kim Kardashian's short marriage (and all the media hoopla that came out of it) easily doubled her profile, her status, her earning power, and her net worth. It's also the promise that your investment will double its value.

And it all starts with 72.

For example, the Rule of 72 shows that $100 invested at 10% would take about 7.2 years [(72/10) = 7.2] to double to $200. In exact math, a 10% investment will take 7.3 years to double [(1.10 x 7.3 = 2].

That's my last Kim Kardashian reference in this book, and it's one more than I had expected to make.

MAKING YOUR MONEY WORK FOR YOU

Putting money in a savings account is predictable and safe, making it a comfortable option for many people. However, currently, we end up getting less than 1% interest per year on most savings accounts, while inflation devalues that money by a few percentage points every year.

Inflation simply means a dollar this year is worth a few cents less than it was a year ago. Over time it's more noticeable, like when our grandparents talk about the cost of a loaf of bread when they were kids. Now we pay more money for the same item.

Technically, the average annual inflation rate from 2003 – 2013 was 2.38%.[66] So if we're collecting less than 1% interest on our savings, and that savings loses buying power by more than 2% per year due to inflation, the overall value of our saved money decreases by 1.38% per year. Your dollar becomes 98.6 cents.

The good news is there are ways to make more money, if you're ready to take risks. You can do this through investing, and there are many ways to do it.

The helpful video "Investing Money in Plain English" by CommonCraft"[67] explains it this way:

Coffee shops are a very common kind of business to open. Let's say you don't want to open one, but your friend does. She needs money to buy materials, like coffee beans, appliances, and a store. She can't pay for all this on her own, so she asks people to invest (give her some money to pay for part of her costs). It's a risk, because you could lose your money if she fails. But if she succeeds, the money you invest in her project could increase.

By giving her money, you become an investor. You now own a percentage of the business (or 'share') equal to your percentage of the overall investing. You're hoping the value of your share increases along with the overall value of the business. This takes time, but you invested because you've decided your money will grow faster in this investment than it would earning a low amount of interest in a savings account.

Savings accounts are safe and predictable because they are federally insured up to $250,000 (banks use Federal Deposit Insurance Certification (FDIC) and credit unions use National Credit Union Administration (NCUA).

They are definitely better than nothing. But if you're ready and willing to take a risk, then investing should be sounding very interesting to you right about now. Remember, your investment could lose value, or gain value, very quickly. This is why investing is, and should always be understood as, a risk.

So that coffee shop story is an example of how the stock market works. When you buy stocks, you're buying a tiny portion of a large business and betting that the business will do well over time, increasing the value of your investment.

You can invest in all kinds of things, not just the stock market or private businesses. You could buy $500 worth of antiques, which may increase in value. In a few years, you may be able to sell them for $750. Or they'll only be worth $400. This is kind of how people went cuh-razy over Beanie Babies in the 90s. Spoiler from the future: that did not work out well for them.

Things always look more clear looking backward, but since you can't go back in time and invest in a winning company (unless you're in every time-travel movie ever made), you have to do your research so that you maximize your reward, not your risk.

And definitely discuss your plans with a financial professional first.

DAY TRADING

Thanks to movies, the most popular version of investing is buying stocks from a Wall Street stockbroker. Think *Wall Street, Glengarry Glen Ross, Boiler Room, The Wolf of Wall Street.* Buying and selling of lots of shares, lots of times.

This activity often more closely resembles gambling than investing. Get-rich-quick dreams are often get-broke-quicker schemes in disguise. We can easily become addicted to the thrill of risk-and-reward, short-circuiting our patience. The extreme version of this is the day trader, who buys and sells stock with a very quick turnaround time. A day trader attempts to profit by making rapid trades, and closing out all trades before the market closes each day. The intention is to sell each stock for more than the purchase price, but that doesn't always work out. The Securities Exchange Commission (SEC) warns that "Day traders typically suffer severe financial losses in their first months of trading, and many never graduate to profit-making status."[68]

For your consideration, here is a less risky philosophy: it's not about *timing* the market as much as it's about *time in* the market. It's about buying stocks and leaving them in for a long time, making common sense adjustments, but not constantly checking your value or making a move because your stock dropped a little bit.

An example of how this works is called *dollar cost averaging*. (If your head is already spinning, you can skip this paragraph.) Dollar cost averaging is the practice of investing the same amount of money in the same investment at regular intervals (like once a month), regardless of what the market is doing. It's an investment principle that isn't influenced by worrying whether you're investing at the "right" or "wrong" time. Dollar cost averaging evens out the ups and downs of the market. As the price of the investment rises, you simply end up purchasing fewer shares because you have chosen to invest the same amount of money each time, and when the price falls, you end up purchasing more. If you've chosen a good place to put your money, you should end up with more, over the course of your investing.

(If you read that last paragraph, way to be a trooper!)

DON'T SCRATCH THAT

Let's clarify something that people often call an investment, but actually isn't: the lottery. It's possible you could buy that one scratch-off ticket that changes your whole life, but the most likely way to win at the lottery is to not play it. The odds of winning are so incredibly low that every single time the game is won, the lottery has turned one person into a millionaire, and millions of others into, well, exactly who they were before, minus the price of their ticket. And the game can go on for weeks and even months before even one person wins.

In fact, the promise of "making millions" in the lottery actually makes more sense if you think of it from the perspective of the lottery organizers: making millions off the losers.

Yet the way the lottery is advertised is far more hope inspiring. One scholar referred to it as "an audacity of hype," saying that lottery advertising's primary aim is to "shift people from hope for social change produced by collective action to hope for personal gain by individual gambling."[69]

And if that wasn't depressing enough, did you know many of the people who have won the lottery have found their lives actually made worse? Their overnight fortune caused division among family and friends, and enabled the winner to spend money completely without self-control. Many lottery winners even end up declaring bankruptcy.

The lottery is a state-run business, and it actually turns a profit despite the huge giveaways. But there are few winners when compared to the number of people who lose, and lose often. Economists across the country provide the facts:

- 68% of lottery winners still participate in the lottery every week, paying money back into the system and decreasing their winnings, while 44% of lottery winners had spent their entire winnings within 5 years.[70]

- The larger the win, the more likely the winner's family will ask for money. Consider the example of Sandra Hayes, who collected $6 million after splitting a $224 million jackpot with coworkers. Hayes stated she "had to endure the greed and the need that people have, trying to get you to release your money to them. That caused a lot of emotional pain. These are people who you've loved deep down, and they're turning into vampires trying to suck the life out of me . . . ... If you're not disciplined, you will go broke. I don't care how much money you have." Winner Evelyn Adams agreed: "Everybody wanted my money. Everybody had his or her hand out. I never learned one simple word in the English language, 'No.' I wish I had the chance to do it all over again. I'd be much smarter about it now."[71]

- The National Endowment for Financial Education estimates that as many as 70% of Americans who experience a sudden windfall will lose that money within a few years.[72]

- A 2010 study showed that poor households (with annual take-home incomes under $13,000) spend on average $645 a year on lottery tickets, which comes to about 9% of their yearly income.[73]

- Households with incomes under $25,000 spent an average of about $600 a year on lottery tickets, while $100,000-plus earners spent about $300 a year. People who never graduated from college spent the most, about $700 a year, while graduates spent under $200.[74]

If the lottery is so negative, why is it so seductive? A 2008 study on risk seeking explored some of the reasons why low-income people spend so much money on lotteries—which are such a bad deal that they make slot machines look good. After exposing the study subjects to certain types of information or experiences, the study's two main conclusions were that "Participants were more likely to purchase lottery tickets when they were primed to perceive that their own income was low relative to an implicit standard . . . " and "Participants purchased more tickets when they considered situations in which rich people or poor people receive advantages, implicitly highlighting the fact that everyone has an equal chance of winning the lottery." [75]

So we take the risk because we're primed to feel that the lottery is the great equalizer of the rich and the poor. On top of that, we're constantly told this vicious cycle is harmless fun. Consider these tag lines:

Massachusetts: Someone's gotta win.
North Dakota: If you don't buy a ticket, how is lady luck going to find you?
Minnesota: What kind of mega millionaire would you be?
Australia: Your ticket to dream.
New York: Hey, you never know!

It's a game. It's fun. You'll feel included. It's the ticket to your dreams. Some lotteries even make the argument that you're supporting your state and contributing to education, since the state uses the money you've lost to finance state projects:

New Mexico: Benefiting New Mexico's Future.

Ohio: Take a chance on education. Odds are, you'll have fun!

New York: Raising billions to educate millions

Great right? As long as you ignore the fact that you are already paying taxes to the state for those things. So the lottery is just giving you the opportunity to pay your taxes twice.

The lottery is a rebrand so bold and brazen, it's almost shocking. Through repetition, the truth is quietly overwhelmed by a thousand positive and pleasant messages inviting you to look at the lottery as something other than a total waste of money.

So if the lottery isn't the way to make money, what is? I'll tell you, and yep, it *does* sound a lot less thrilling: saving gradually over time to reach your goal.

AFFORDING A PORCH TO ROCK ON

It may seem far away from now, especially if you're in the beginning of your career, but someday you'll need to retire, meaning you'll live without income from a job.

In 2010's movie *Live Free or Die Hard*, John McClane (now a bit more lumbering at age sixty), gets singled out by a techno-hacker who figures out his identity and then wipes out his pension.[76] His IRA, his 401K, and his police pension are all gone. How is he supposed to retire now? I guess he can always be the crankiest greeter at Wal-Mart.

More importantly, how are those of us who don't have stunt doubles or multi-film contracts, and thus can never die, supposed to retire? Retirement is a period of your life when you stop working and use the money you've saved to pay for the last part of your life.

And it turns out that it's all in the approach. You have to make a plan and put it to work. It will not take care of itself.

First, let's apply the magic of compound interest to saving for retirement. You'll see that the best thing you can do is start early. Here's an example: Two people put $2,000 a year into a retirement account (the limit allowed is $5,000, but we'll say it was $2,000). Ben started saving this much at age 19 and stopped contributing to the account at age 26. Arthur started at age 27, and even though he contributes every year for 37 years, he NEVER CATCHES UP TO BEN!

AGE	BEN		ARTHUR	
19	2,000	2,240	0	0
20	2,000	4,749	0	0
21	2,000	7,558	0	0
22	2,000	10,706	0	0
23	2,000	14,230	0	0
24	2,000	18,178	0	0
25	2,000	22,599	0	0
26	2,000	27,551	0	0
27	0	30,857	2,000	2,240
28	0	34,560	2,000	4,749
29	0	38,708	2,000	7,558
30	0	43,352	2,000	10,706
31	0	48,554	2,000	14,230
32	0	54,381	2,000	18,178
33	0	60,907	2,000	22,599
34	0	68,216	2,000	27,551
35	0	76,802	2,000	33,097
36	0	85,570	2,000	39,309
37	0	95,383	2,000	46,266
38	0	107,339	2,000	54,058
39	0	120,220	2,000	62,785
40	0	134,646	2,000	72,559
41	0	150,804	2,000	83,506

AGE	BEN		ARTHUR	
42	0	168,900	2,000	95,767
43	0	189,168	2,000	109,499
44	0	211,869	2,000	124,879
45	0	237,293	2,000	142,104
46	0	265,768	2,000	161,396
47	0	297,660	2,000	183,004
48	0	333,379	2,000	207,204
49	0	373,385	2,000	234,308
50	0	418,191	2,000	264,665
51	0	468,374	2,000	298,665
52	0	524,579	2,000	336,745
53	0	587,528	2,000	379,394
54	0	658,032	2,000	427,161
55	0	736,995	2,000	480,660
56	0	825,435	2,000	540,579
57	0	924,487	2,000	607,688
58	0	1,035,425	2,000	682,851
59	0	1,159,676	2,000	767,033
60	0	1,298,837	2,000	861,317
61	0	1,454,698	2,000	966,915
62	0	1,629,261	2,000	1,085,185
63	0	1,824,773	2,000	1,217,647
64	0	2,043,746	2,000	1,366,005
65	0	**2,288,996**	2,000	**1,532,166**

That result is called the *time value of money*. In the first few years of compound interest, Ben's investment has grown to a point where it adds more every year than the $2,000 Arthur puts in. You can't beat starting early. (The above example is an ideal version of this, just to be clear.)

But if you are in your late twenties or older when you start saving for retirement, don't be discouraged. Do it anyway. Remember this proverb: "The best time to plant a tree was twenty years ago. The next best time is today."

Here are the kinds of retirement accounts you can consider:

Traditional Individual Retirement Account (IRA): An IRA is a tax-deferred retirement account for an individual, meaning you can contribute money to it each year, and you aren't taxed on it until you start withdrawing it at age 59 1/2 or later. The taxes are not paid each year with contribution, but at time of withdrawal, when you may be taxed at a lower rate, as well.

Roth Individual Retirement Account (IRA): A special retirement account where you pay taxes on the money you contribute to your retirement when you contribute it, so that when you withdraw it in retirement you won't be taxed on it. If are starting your career or making a lower income than you will when you're older, this allows you to pay taxes on future income at the lower rate you have now instead of later when that money has grown larger.[77]

401(k): An employer-sponsored plan, the 401(k) allows employees to set aside a portion of their paycheck taxes-deferred (meaning to be paid later) in investment plans for retirement purposes. In some cases employers will match the employees contribution as much as dollar for dollar. But withdrawing some of the funds before you reach a certain specified age will trigger a penalty tax.

Simplified Employee Pension (SEP): For self-employed people or owners of companies with less than twenty-five employees, an SEP allows them to defer taxes on investments intended for retirement. It allows them to contribute much more than the limits usually applied to Roth, IRA, or 401(k). In an SEP you can contribute up to 25% of your adjusted gross income at the end of the year, or up to certain specified dollar limits, whichever is less. This is a great way to increase the amount of money in your retirement account that you want to be collecting interest over the course of your career.

This is a great subject to discuss with a financial adviser, and many financial advisers offer free consultations to explain all this to you, in exchange for the chance to be hired by you to manage your investments. You're under no obligation to buy anything after a free consultation, and it's a great way to ask questions, go deeper, and really grasp this stuff. You can even apply what you learn to a self-managed account, where the fees may be lower but the decisions are up to you. This is an easy subject to feel dumb about, but remember, it's your money. You can learn this, and it will get less intimidating the more you work on it. So the most important thing is: don't put it off. Ask questions, get involved, and down the road you'll reap the rewards.

APPENDIX

QUICK GUIDE: BUYING A CAR

"Wherever we want to go, we go. That's what a ship is, you know. It's not just a keel and a hull and sails; that's what a ship needs. What the Black Pearl really is, is freedom."

—Jack Sparrow, *The Pirates of the Caribbean: Curse of the Black Pearl*

You never forget your first car. My parents bought me my first car as a high school graduation present.

That makes me sound like a rich kid. To be clear, it was a $400 Dodge Omni. For which I'll always be grateful, since $400 sounded like a million dollars at the time. I loved having a car of my own. It was freedom and independence. As it turns out, it was also a stick shift. Which meant I had no idea how to drive it.

It was pretty strange to own a car and not be able to get it out of the driveway. Since my stepdad was working out of town during the week, for a few weeks that car just sat there. I was ready to trade it in for something else, although I'm not sure what I thought $400 was going to get me on the car market. Maybe a set of tires with no car to put them on.

After a few weeks, I convinced a friend to teach me to drive stick shift. I spent the next few hours jamming down the clutch, slamming it into gear, and letting off the clutch while awkwardly lurching forward or stalling, and also revving the gas for no reason. Eventually I got the hang of it.

By learning to drive stick shift, I learned a skill for life, one that would allow me to buy cars with longer lasting, reliable transmissions, often at more affordable prices. Those are the key words when it comes to buying a car: reliable and affordable. Safe and smart.

A car is not a cheap decision. Unless you're an antique car collector, a car is a liability (meaning something that only takes money out of your life, and doesn't bring in any). It also has ongoing costs, such as insurance, gas, and repairs. So it's a really good purchase to think through carefully.

Keep in mind, that when it comes to money, a great rule of thumb is this: the bigger the purchase, the bigger the chance to save.

Below are the four phases of buying a reliable, affordable used car.

PHASE 1: THE PLAN

When you start looking for a car, you'll quickly find out just how many cars are out there! It's good to help yourself by making a few pre-search decisions. If you want to find a dependable car at an affordable price, you have to outline your deal-breakers first. What do you absolutely NOT want?

What are yours?

Personally, I would never drive a car that's also an ice cream truck. If it has the word "ding-a-ling" on it, I don't want to be seen in it. But that's just me. In reality, 'deal-breaker' is just a negative way of describing a requirement. Here are five really important requirements:

1) You have a good test drive.
   Easy start? Engine sounds good? No weird noises? Brakes work well? We'll talk more about this in Phase 3: The Test.

2) It runs a clean Carfax report.
   The site www.carfax.com is where you can see the registered history of the car, listed by its vehicle identification number (VIN). You can see if it's been in any accidents, and what maintenance has been done. The website will give you the option of buying one or five reports, and though it's more money, I recommend paying for five. You'll want to run a Carfax report on every car you look at.

3) The final price is something you can afford.
   It's not just the sticker price. There's the total price

after paying interest if you're getting a lease, as well as registration, maintenance, and insurance. You could also call a prospective insurance company and ask them what insurance they would you offer on this type of car and why. That can be a good way to find out how safe the car is, and what costs are associated with it.

4) Your mechanic approves the car.

You can ask the seller to let your mechanic evaluate the car, and drive it to her or his auto shop. This evaluation can cost fifty dollars or so. This way you get the opinion of an objective third party, and you find out if the car will pass its next inspection. That fifty dollars could save you thousands down the road by saving you from buying the wrong car.

5) It has good reviews from other owners.

Kelly Blue Book or www.KBB.com is where you can look up the Blue Book Value of the car. That's the current sale value of the car. You can also look up the car in Consumer Reports to see their safety rating.

PHASE 2: THE SEARCH

When you're searching for a car, searching online will help you cut down on your trip time going to check out and drive cars.

Sites like www.cars.com, www.usedcars.com, www. autotrader.com, and www.craigslist.org (actually pretty reputable for car searching because dealers post their ads there as well) are a good start.

An auction is also a great place to see a bunch of cars in one day. Personally, I like auctions because it's one of the few places you can see an old man wearing both a cowboy hat and a fanny pack. But it has a downside, too: it's designed for quick decisions. You can't test drive the car, and you can't have your mechanic inspect the car first.

The auctioneers will encourage you to get into a bidding war, pitting you against other interested parties. It's a fast-paced, emotional environment. If you go early and really know what you're doing, you could do well. But if you don't like the idea of becoming the owner of a car you've never seen before in less than the length of a Bingo round, an auction probably isn't going to be your best search option. You could end up with a car you really don't want. But it is a fun experience, and you'll get to see a lot of cars in one day.

During the rest of your search time, you'll probably be checking out cars from private sellers and dealers.

PHASE 3: THE TEST

In this section I'll connect you to some tools to make sure the car passes your test, and to help you think about the environment in which you're buying your car. You might be talking to a private seller or a dealer. Car dealers/salespeople get a bad rap. We tend to think of their job as "selling cars they're lying about." That may be true in some cases, but I've met many honest car salespeople. Rather than being overly suspicious or overly trusting, it's better to evaluate each one on a case-by-case basis, and keep in mind some of the approaches they implement when doing their job.

If you were a car salesman, what would you want your customers to think about you? You'd want them to think you're telling the truth. It would be to your advantage to earn their trust and build rapport.

Here are some of the things car salesmen said to me to spark a little chemistry:

> *"I want you to be happy with this car."*
> *"If anything at all goes wrong with this car, you can bring it here and we'll help you out."* (Meaning, bring it to their repair shop.)
> *"Whatever you need my friend, I'm happy to provide."*
> *"I got into this business to make sure people get an honest deal."*

"At this price, I'll just be breaking even on this car."

Car dealers try to build a connection with you, the buyer, and you can use these same kinds of strategies on them.

Notice the use of the phrase "my friend." Often a seller will try to make you feel like you're connecting, then introduce tension by being offended when your conversation comes around to the price you want to pay. It's simply a strategy. And at the end of the day, you are the one who has more at stake here. You want a car you can rely on for years to come. So it pays to be thorough and patient, and not fall in love with any vehicle too quickly.

Always do a test drive, and bring a thorough test-drive checklist like this one www.balancepro.net/education/pdf/usedcartestdrive.pdf with you to make sure you're looking at the right details on your test drive.

Another tip: be sure to read every line of the warranty. You might find that some critical things that cost the most to replace are actually not covered, like brakes, gaskets, and transmissions.

PHASE 4: THE PURCHASE

What is the best time to buy a car? If you live in a four-season climate, the answer is winter.

Why? Well, a few reasons. The most obvious one is cold weather. Fewer people are out looking for cars this time of year. There are also other things going on. November through December is the holiday season, which means while everyone is out holiday shopping, they're not looking for cars. The coldest part of the year means slower sales, which has sellers itching for a sale. And at the end of the month, most sales associates have a sales quota they are trying to meet, so they're more motivated to compromise a little on their price.

A key part of car buying is negotiating with the seller. Everyone has his or her own style for "haggling."

You could yell at them until they do what you want, but that's probably not that effective. So before we close out this section, let's try a quick negotiation exercise. Let's say you are a seller—what are some tricks you might try to get a higher price out of your buyer?

You could create a connection with the buyer, then break the connection by appearing offended. Manipulate emotions.

You could ask them how much they are looking to spend. The person who says a price first usually loses, because they've anchored the conversation at a certain place, and they're not going to get the price below that, even if the car is worth less.

When you are buying a car from a seller or dealer, it's important to be strategic when it comes to discussing price. You're often negotiating with someone who negotiates for a living.

Here are three common strategies car sellers use when negotiating, including one I already referenced in Phase 3:

1) Who Draws First: They say the person who gives a number first is usually the one who loses. Here's when that isn't the case: by stating the first number, you can create an anchor point for the discussion. So it pays to keep it on the low side, less than the maximum amount you'd be willing to pay. All following prices can be relative to your first number. Your biggest benefit comes from paying attention to the person's reaction when you start talking numbers, and trying to gauge whether you're in their ballpark. (I realize this contradicts the advice I gave earlier about not saying your price first. What I'm trying to show you is that it's up to you to experiment and find your style.)

2) Bump & Grind: It's not just for late-90s dance floors anymore. The bump and grind is where a seller will slightly bump up your price by adding

a new feature. If you agree, they'll see an opportunity to keep doing so. They'll bump up the price in small amounts through add-on services they think you'll be attracted to, in order to grind away your dedication to the maximum you're willing to spend. Yes, this was still awkward to explain.

3) The Temperature Drop: A car purchase can be like a mini-relationship, where the seller focuses on creating an emotional connection with you at first, and then becomes offended when you lowball them on price. Remember, you can do The Temperature Drop, too. Remember, also, you can always walk away—you're not going to offend anybody, and you'll probably win their respect by sticking to your price. They won't tell you that though.

Once you've settled on a price for the car, you still need to watch out for add-ons. This is when you might meet the Finance and Insurance Officer (or Business Manager), usually the highest paid salesperson in the dealership.

FINANCING:

Your best bet is to pay for the car in cash, or get pre-approved financing from a financial institution before you go to a car dealership. If the dealer's in-house financing can beat the rate you already have, well that's even better for you. But you'll have the advantage of knowing that the reward for doing your homework was a better rate and therefore a lower payment.

GETTING A LOAN

Shop around at local lenders like banks and credit unions.

A loan application will ask for:
- Employment history
- Income
- Debts

You'll need to provide:
- Recent Paystubs
- Proof of insurance
- Vehicle information
- Possible money down or a co-signer or borrower

The lender will pull your credit report and credit score to determine how well you can be expected to repay the loan.

So while some of these skills may seem foreign at first—like learning to negotiate with a seasoned pro—if you're willing to give it a try, and not just stick with what you already know, it'll pay off.

And it will continue to make a difference for years to come.

QUICK GUIDE: HIGHER EDUCATION

According to the US Bureau of Labor Statistics (BLS), 68% of high school students attend college.[78] "College" means some form of education or certification beyond high school.

It's important to remember that the term "college" doesn't only mean a four-year, private university or college. It's really an umbrella term for a variety of post-secondary training: certification, apprenticeship, community college, commuter college, private college, public university, associate's degree, bachelor's degree, master's degree, doctorate.

Here are definitions for the different types of higher education from Big Future:[79]

Universities: often larger and offer more majors and degree options than colleges (bachelor's, master's, and doctoral degrees); most contain several smaller colleges; prepare you for a variety of careers or for graduate study.

Four-year colleges: (include universities and liberal arts colleges) four-year programs that lead to a bachelor's degree.

Two-year colleges: (include community colleges, vocational-technical colleges, and career colleges) offer programs that last up to two years that lead to a certificate or an associate's degree.

Public colleges: funded by local and state

governments; usually offer lower tuition rates, especially for state residents.

Private colleges: funded by tuition, fees, and private funding sources; can sometimes provide generous financial aid.

For-profit colleges: businesses offering degree programs for specific careers; tend to have higher costs; credits earned may not transfer to other colleges.

Liberal arts colleges: offer broad base of courses in areas such as literature, history, languages, mathematics, and life sciences; usually private with four-year programs leading to bachelor's degree; prepare you for a variety of careers or for graduate study.

It's really healthier for us to talk about higher education as the umbrella set of options that it is, otherwise you might think you have to go to a four-year institution or you're not getting as viable an education as you need. In reality, almost 40% of students who begin four-year college programs don't complete them, which can translate into a whole lot of wasted time, wasted money, and burdensome student loan debt.

Of those who do finish college, 33% or more will end up in jobs they could have had without a four-year degree. Statistics indicate that 37% of currently employed college grads are doing work for which only a high school diploma is required.

CREDIT CARDS AND COLLEGE

By the time you reach post-high-school education, you are old enough for credit card debt and credit card tricks to really come into play in your life. Credit card access and availability skyrockets when you become an adult. It's been estimated that the average freshman gets eight credit card offers in their first week of college. Before the federal Credit Card Act of 2009 restricted this practice, credit card tables at orientation events and career fairs were the norm. Now around 18% of students get their credit card through tabling at an event, and 52% get one through direct mail.[80]

A 2008 survey referenced on Debt.org revealed that seniors graduate with an average debt of more than $4,100 in consumer expenses paid for on a card: food, going out, gas, and small purchases.[81] Also according to that study, close to one in five seniors have credit card debt of more than $7,000. Scary stuff.

Fortunately, thanks to the implementation of the Credit Card Accountability Responsibility and Disclosure Act (C.A.R.D.) (see what they did there?) of 2009, SallieMae reported that college seniors in 2014 graduate with around $610 in credit card debt.[82]

In our culture, the debt acquired in college is for many people the beginning of decades of debt. In a phone survey of 1,007 adults conducted by the organization

GfK Roper in 2013, 9% of Americans answered the question, "When do you expect to be debt free?" by answering "never."

The average age of predicted debt freedom was 53.

People start out being optimistic, but over time, the prediction of debt freedom keeps advancing. People aged 18-24 are the most optimistic, with an average prediction of debt freedom at about age 33; but 25-34 year olds predict age 38; next, 35-49 year olds predict age 56; then, 50-64 year olds predict age 62 (just a reminder that this is an average, otherwise that number wouldn't compute coming from a 64 year old!); and at age 65-plus, debt freedom is expected, on average, at age 77.[83]

So, personal debt is definitely worth having a strategy to pay off. Like the one I gave you at the end of Chapter 4: Take Charge of Your Debt. And despite it being an incredibly common experience, most people don't want to talk openly about it.

In a 2013 CreditCards.com phone survey, 1,005 participants were asked, "How likely would you be to talk openly to someone you've just met about this topic?" and then they were given a series of subjects. The most taboo topic: the amount of your credit card debt (85% would not talk about it). This scored above "details of your love life" (84%), "your salary" (80%), and way above "your political views" (49%) and "your views about religion" (41%).[84]

So on a first date, people would rather talk about politics, religion, and exes than talk about debt.

The article then makes a really fantastic point:

Larry Compeau, professor of consumer behavior at Clarkson University in Potsdam, N.Y., said he's not surprised that several of the most-unmentionable topics relate to money. America's Protestant work ethic culture means that much of our identity is tied up in how we're doing financially so not being able to provide for your family or pay the bills can cause feelings of embarrassment and shame.

Compeau recently saw that firsthand, when he conducted in-depth interviews for a research project with consumers who had suffered major debt problems. 'One person I interviewed was deeply religious and said he talked to his pastor about everything, including his wife's infidelity,' Compeau said. 'But when he ran into financial problems, he wasn't comfortable sharing that with his pastor.'

Part of the problem, Compeau said, is that even though there are legitimate reasons people go into debt (medical bills, job loss), the American culture tends to assume that if you're having financial trouble, it's your own fault and you have some kind of character flaw.

This tendency to blame people for their debt is called the Fundamental Attribution Error, wherein we tend to assume that our own actions are justified, because we are motivated by outside pressures. For example, "I ran that red light because I'm late for a meeting." But when evaluating other people's actions, we assume they are motivated more by their natures. For example, "She or he ran that red light because she or he is an idiot."

That's why it's really important to give yourself grace. Our ability to talk about our problems is a critical step in solving them. Talking creates connection, empathy, and validation. It also often prompts advice and encouragement from others. What goes unsaid often reinforces the shame that caused us not to talk about it in the first place.

"COLLEGE IS GOOD DEBT"

The expression "college is *good* debt" is actually why we're breaking down the concept of debt. Paying debt off is just a task for which we need to form a plan.

College debt doesn't negatively affect your credit score (unless you don't pay it back), because you are improving your payable skills. It's considered an investment in yourself. While this is true, and it's important that our system has built in some protections for you as a borrower since you are funding your education, the reality is that there is no good debt. Good debt is not having any.

Credit is good; debt, not good.

Debt is an important thing to deliver yourself from. And even though more students drop out of college because of financial pressure than because of their grade point average, it still holds that college graduates earn 84% more over their lifetimes than people without college degrees.[85] College graduates earn $570,000 more than high school graduates over a lifetime.[86] College graduates are more satisfied in their jobs. And college graduates are less likely to smoke and more likely to exercise.[87]

In 2013 the typical worker with less than a high school diploma was estimated to earn $973,000 over the course of their career. That seems like a lot of money, but over fifty years that's $19,640 a year. The typical professional (doctor or lawyer) will earn $3.6 million. College graduates fall halfway between.[88]

On such a hot-button issue, with millions of jobs resting on the importance of college existing, and millions of students going into debt and then struggling to find work despite their college degree, of course there are passionate and well-made arguments on both sides. Some argue that college is still a good investment, with the only real negative being the wages students forego while in college.[89]

Others point out that college costs have increased at three times the rate of inflation every year in recent years.[90] And student debt has skyrocketed since the beginning of 2005.[91] Total US student loan debt now exceeds $1 trillion.[92] Student loan debt now tops credit card debt among Americans.[93]

Yet throughout this process, the rhetoric around college has been slow to change.

The tension is this: colleges are businesses that survive by making money, yet are staffed by people who want to help you reach your best possible future. They are neither all good nor all bad. However, the rhetoric surrounding the need for college tends to oversimplify their role pretty powerfully, to where they're either crooks or they'll save your life.

Colleges definitely benefit from a cultural sense of necessity. The best businesses sell their product to you through the buy-in of your peers and parents. Colleges are not different. Parents pressure you to go to college. Your friends feel the pressure to go somewhere. Your high school teachers tell you that you need a college education if you want a job. When I was in high school, I ended up feeling like I was supposed to go to college, no questions asked.

"JUST GO TO COLLEGE"

In the 2006 movie *Accepted*, a group of high school graduates finds out they weren't accepted to any of the colleges
they applied to. For some people, college postpones that
wave of reality that comes when you stop going to school
and choose where you will enter the world of work. This
movie focuses on the pressure students face to make college their next step—instead of work—even when they
don't know what it'll do for their lives.

In the movie, over dinner, Bartleby tries to explain
to his parents that he didn't get in to any colleges, and
why that's not necessarily a bad thing.

> Bartleby: Okay, I figure it like this. The average cost
> of college is, what, $20,000 a year? Now, accord-
> ing to these estimates that I got off the Web. (You
> can pass those around.) Someone with no educa-
> tion beyond high school can expect to make about
> $20,000 a year in the current job market. Now, that
> being said, over the next four years, you could either
> spend $80,000 or I could make $80,000.
>
> Dad: Okay, cut the crap, Bartleby. Society has
> rules. And the first rule is, you go to college. You
> want to have a happy and successful life? You go to
> college. If you want to be somebody, you go to col-
> lege. If you want to fit in, you go to college.[94]

That kind of selling pressure, coming from parents, is very powerful. College is doing well when it turns parents into unpaid sales associates.

College *is* a business, but so are you. You get to make the choice that's right for you. Not going to college will save you a lot of money, but going to college will improve your earning power. In a report released in 2013, "Education Pays," researchers break down, by education level, an individual's estimated cumulative lifetime annual earnings (in 2011 dollars), after repaying tuition fees. The report shows that by age 34 an associate's degree recipient will have earned more than a high school diploma recipient. At age 36, the bachelor's degree recipient passes the high school diploma recipient. At age 37, the bachelor's degree recipient passes the associate's degree recipient. By age 64, the bachelor's degree recipient has out earned the high school diploma recipient by $303,531.[95] (Interesting to note that an associate's degree spikes more quickly over the short term, but can't sustain compared to a bachelor's over the long term.)

Clearly *not* going to college can save you money, especially if you don't know why you're going there.

So can approaching college with a financial plan, which will help you save thousands of dollars. The bigger the purchase, the bigger opportunity to save. Your third option is to go for the increased earning power over the course of your career. How do you choose? Ultimately, it comes down to one very important question: why am *I* going to college?

WHY AM *I* GOING TO COLLEGE?

Think about this: what if you could go on a cruise where you meet some of the best people you've ever met, and you have some of the most fun nights of your life? You laugh, you party, you learn, you might fall in love. One day that ship reaches shore, and you have to get off the ship. And then you pay every month for the next ten to twenty years for that experience.

If you're going to college because you don't know what else to do with your life, you're on the ship. If you're going to find great friends and maybe fall in love, you're on the ship.

I was definitely on the ship. My parents told me not to go if I didn't know what field I wanted to work in. I went anyway, and made some of the best friends I'd ever had, and fell in love a few times, too. I did fine in my classes, but they were not my #1 priority. Wouldn't you know it; after graduating I still didn't know what I wanted to do. I floated around trying on a lot more jobs than I might have had to before I found a field I saw a future in.

By going to college with no idea or plan, you're paying to find out what you want to do, when you could be getting people to pay you to find out what you want—by getting jobs and internships.

After graduating, I discovered that the very expensive private college I attended didn't have much name recognition with employers. All they saw from my resume was that I had a college degree. This is an important thing to think about: are the employers in the industry you want to pursue interested in where you got your degree, or simply that you got one?

To answer this, make a phone call to someone in the Human Resources (HR) or hiring department of a company in a field that interests you. Ask them what schools they think are best for this field, and if they favor four-year degrees over two-year degrees in applicants. With a phone call or two, you might just save yourself a lot of money and a lot of time choosing the right school and the best program for your education. And you can always call them again when you graduate and tell them their advice changed your life, and oh by the way you're a graduate now.

Another great way to spend less on college is by looking at community colleges. They are a fantastic resource, allowing you to spend less money while you put your college education together, and figure out what you are going to do next. Community colleges offer things like certificate programs and associate's degrees. Also, your coursework can transfer to a four-year institution, if you decide that's what you want. So you can save money on courses for those two years, get an associate's degree, and move on to a four-year school without missing a beat.

Rather than going to college to figure out what you want to do and spending money to try things out, consider an alternative. Many countries advocate taking a "gap year," a time to work, travel, take a year off from school, and get a sense of what you might want to get out of college, if you do go. That's valuable information to have, and a lot of students in America are starting to give serious thought to something many European students have done for years.

I went directly to college after high school, and I denied myself that real-life experience I could have used. I was in college not to plan out the next phase of my life, but to pretend it wasn't going to arrive. That's a shame because I know now that life after school is this big, beautiful place where you have so much time to try different things, change directions, and search for what you most want to do.

I went to a private liberal arts college, and I spent hundreds of dollars per credit to take required general education classes that weren't relevant to my major. The most striking example is a class called "Introduction to Visual Arts." It was the second of two ninety-minute classes I attended first thing in the morning. I'd make it through the first class all right, and then in the fifteen-minute break between classes, lack of sleep caught up with me. I'd go to "Visual Arts" and the teacher would turn all the lights off and speak in a monotone about thousands of slides of art. My goal was to stay awake for at least the first ten minutes. Now that's money well spent.

One time I fell asleep with my feet propped against this metal divider, and I had a dream that I was falling out of my chair. I popped awake and pulled my feet down to the floor but the heels of my shoes had hooked onto this little metal lip, so when I jerked my feet away, they recoiled and drove forward into the metal divider. I basically kicked the divider with both feet full-force, like a ninja in zero gravity. It created a sound like thunder. It was impossibly loud. Everyone in class started laughing except for the teacher, who paused for about two seconds, clicked the next slide, and continued to drone.

Those were the most expensive and stressful naps I've ever taken.

I remained "Undeclared" in my major for the first full two years of college, and even though I chose a Communications major for my last two years, I constantly questioned if that's what I wanted to do. And when I graduated, I had no concept of how to get a job in my field. I spent a few years taking any job I could, trying to make some money and pay my bills. Not the worst life, but definitely confusing, since I wasn't using my major. It wasn't until four years after graduation that I found work connected to my major.

And that's true for too many people.

According to a CareerBuilder survey of 2,134 workers in 2014, 47% of college graduates did not find a first job that was related to their college major. And 32% of college grads said they had never worked in a field related to their majors.[96]

There's often a sense of disconnection between college and career life, when in reality, college could be the first on-point chapter of your career. You can't rush into that if you don't know what you want to do yet. So take some time, a gap year or classes at a community college—get your general education requirements out of the way as you experiment with what you'd like to be doing next.

HOW MUCH TO BORROW?

When borrowing money for college, one rule of thumb is: don't borrow more for college than you expect to earn in your first year out of school.

To make that specific you would use a loan repayment calculator like the one on www.finaid.gov, or look up your career prospect on www.salary.com. Both will tell you what you can expect to make in a particular job at entry-level. For an ad-free option, try the Bureau of Labor Statistics career exploration website: www.bls.gov/k12/content/students/careers/career-exploration.htm.

There's also a more specific rule you could look at: your student loan payments should not exceed 8-12% of the monthly income you expect to be earning once you are out on your own.

If you are earning $40,000, that salary comes to $3,333 a month. Computing 8-12% of that comes out to payments of between $266 and $400 a month. (Other examples: $30,000 = $200-300 a month; $60,000 = $400-600 a month).[97]

Seventy-one percent of students graduate from college with some debt.[98] The average national debt for a graduating college senior in 2012 was $29,400. No small chunk. And that's a 25% increase over $23,450 just four years earlier.[99]

Let's get a sense of what it looks like to pay this off monthly. So take $29,400, and go to Finaid.gov's loan repayment calculator: http://www.finaid.org/calculators/loanpayments.phtml. At an interest rate of 6.8%, the payment for a debt of $29,400 is $338 every month for ten years. Ouch. If you're thinking that's more than you want to spend per month, let's pay it back over 20 years. That now becomes $224 a month. And it also means you'll be paying around $24,450 in interest over the 20 years—or nearly as much again as you borrowed in the first place.

LIVING WITH LOANS, NOT ON THEM

This really is a bummer, isn't it? Student debt isn't something we talk about even after we incur the debt, because when I give you these numbers, chances are you'll feel anxious. Psychologically, the effect of debt on most people is actually to shop, thus creating more debt. People medicate that panic, that confusion, with more foolish purchases with their money.

They surrender to their fate.

If you feel like surrendering because you already have that debt, your response should not be "I'm already in the hole, it's not going to make much difference if I keep digging." It's easy to feel that way, but you need to stay positive; you need to form a plan; and you need to start paying in small increments as soon as you can. Start climbing rather than keep digging.

You need to live *with* your loans, not live *on* them.

A friend of mine in medical school is currently paying huge amounts of money to get her degree. One day, she rolls up in an expensive new car and says, "Well, I'm already in so much debt anyway." This is totally understandable. It's also heading in the wrong direction. Very subtly, she's choosing to keep digging.

Think of it as a battle—how are you going to get back to zero as fast as you can? These are your years to live lean, cut corners, and keep your expenses low so you can pay that debt off. Once you have, you can move on to the next chapter in your life and start accumulating some significant savings.

BATTLE BACK TO ZERO

When it comes to your student loans, stay positive and keep on paying them off. Pay off whatever you can, whenever you can. Talk to your financial aid department and start coming up with a plan. There are repayment plans you can ask about, like Income-Based Repayment, Graduated-Repayment, Loan Forgiveness, and more. If you have one hundred dollars you can spare to pay into your student loans, go for it. Don't necessarily assume that way down the road this is all going to be taken care of and you'll have a killer job with a huge salary. You want to start forming the habits now that will allow you to get out of debt, get on with your life, and make it a great one.

Save up whatever you can to pay off your debt as soon as you get your first bill. Can you put aside $500 or $1000? Whatever amount you put aside means you'll be that much closer to being debt-free.

I know lots of people who've finally paid off their loan debt, and now they have a degree, a good job, and can start really loading up their net worth by saving money. Chase that day in your own life, because when it happens to you it will all have been worth it.

QUICK GUIDE: MINI-PHILANTHROPY

There is a far more powerful achievement than making money, and that's making a difference.

If you want to become a mini-humanitarian (and many people do), the good news is that making money can help you make the world a better place. Another fantastic benefit of my own budgeting and figuring out how much I could afford to give away was sponsoring a child.

Which parents would agree is *not* quite as challenging as having a child. His name is Ever, he's eight years old, and he lives in El Salvador. It's very low maintenance parenting.

Ever's awesome. Even though the agency told me they'd translate my letter to him into Spanish, I felt I didn't need it. Why? I took Spanish in high school. So I feel like I still got it. I *comprehendiando*.

This last time I wrote Ever a letter, I got a picture from him in return. Which was nice, but I thought it was strange, so I decided to translate the letter I'd already sent to this kid. Here is what I wrote:

"Dear Ever de Jesus, how are you?"
(So far so good.)
"My Spanish is very pregnant."
(So that's awkward right away.)

"Which you can see from this quick little fart."

(I think I meant note.)

"Obviousmente."

(Which is not a word in either language. Google basically said, "I don't know, man.")

"You have always been my tallest grandfather."

"What old is you?"

(That's a great question if you ever want to stop a conversation cold. Just ask someone, "What old is you?")

"The animal drinks seawater deliciously."

(What? This letter has taken a strange turn. The reading level has jumped. One minute I'm talking about farts, the next thing I'm Ernest Hemingway. Ernesto Hemingway, perhaps.)

"I like colors."

(Oh good, I sound stupid again. That didn't take long.)

"Why is the phone number that we would wish to be is your favorite?"

(Still waiting for an answer on that one.)

"I am a library."

(This is adorable. And it's time to wrap it up.)

"Well, good beans Ever. Enjoy fun."

(Because it's impossible not to. Really think about that—have you ever not enjoyed fun?)

I learned three things from this exchange of messages.

1) I can make anything awkward, even charity.

2) That this eight-year-old sponsored child took one look at my letter and thought, "This grown man is a moron." So he downgraded me to pictures with basic shapes, primary colors, and things I might understand.

3) While my linguistic contributions may have not have factored much into Ever's life, my money is helping meet Ever's needs. And that makes me happy every time I think about it.

As someone who has always had to work hard to make money, I can still make a small sacrifice that allows me to make a difference in someone else's life. Giving money away has changed the way I see money.

WHAT MAKES A HUMANITARIAN?

Our relationship to money affects us in all kinds of significant ways. It also affects the people around us. It allows us to practice self-control, achieve seemingly impossible dreams, make a life for ourselves, and make a difference for others.

It makes me very proud to live in a world where some of our most successful people, the Muhammad Alis and Bill Gateses of the world, are known almost as much for their philanthropy as they are for their wealth.

Did you know that wrestler John Cena has granted over 500 Make-A-Wishes?[100] Just thinking about that makes me smile.

It's easy to think that once we're highly successful ourselves, then we'll be able to give back and help others. Generally, that's true. Planning to become more successful so you can become more generous makes a lot of sense. I think a good giving philosophy is similar to the advice a friend of mine gives when she teaches First Aid to ambulance squads. Every time she asked a new class what the first rule of First Aid is, they'd always say things like "Check the airway," or "Look for bleeding." But the first rule of first aid, is make sure you are OK and not in any danger yourself, so you can take care of other people safely.

If you don't take care of yourself, you can't help others. Once you've stabilized your own money situation, you can give back in a meaningful way for a long time to come. But while you're working on reaching the heights you aspire to, there are plenty of smaller opportunities that prove you don't need a lot of money in order to make an impact and still stay on course.

Let's consider the following intoxicating possibility: good money habits generate more money for us to give. They also bring us the flexibility to pursue meaningful, non-paying work like volunteering for charities, joining a government commission or the board of directors for a nonprofit, or running for political office. There is important work that needs to be done, even if it doesn't pay well or at all. And then, good money habits give us life experience, both mistakes and successes, which allow us to offer our own money advice to others. We can write a better money story with our lives.

Let's acknowledge for a minute that if you've ever been asked to give money, that moment can feel a little strange. Whether the request is from a homeless person on the street, or a cashier who asks you to round up your purchase to benefit a charitable cause, the thought of giving brings up all kinds of feelings in people.

For some, it's easy—they just make the donation, and go about their business. For others, it might bring out a lack of sympathy: "Why should I give you what I worked hard to earn?" For others it's a lack of resources, which can feel a bit shaming: "I wish I could help, but I barely have enough for myself."

In all likelihood, either of the last two can make you feel a bit uncertain about yourself. "Am I a good person? Am I greedy? Am I actually compassionate, or do I just pretend I am?"

I've struggled with this myself.

Back when I started the journey toward becoming a financial speaker, I was afraid that studying money would change me. I thought thinking about it too much would make me more materialistic. But after years of thinking and talking and pondering and analyzing the world of money, I haven't changed the way I feared I would change.

My values look a lot like they did before. I still find joy in things that have nothing to do with money. The main thing I learned is that paying attention to your money is *not* a dangerous step toward falling in love with it. It's an important step toward having a *better* relationship with it. It's a valuable step toward the life you want, and toward figuring out for yourself what it means to truly live.

Money itself is not the corrupting force, our reaction to it is. The need for money is very different from greed for money, and giving is our best weapon against greed. Money is simply a tool to bring you happiness and fulfillment. One of the ways it brings us happiness is when we give it away.

Unfortunately, living in a culture of consumption means that we are subtly trained to do the exact opposite. The message we hear thousands of times a day is a lot more *get* than *give*.

BECOMING A MINI-PHILANTHROPIST

Looking back, most of the time I was told I should be giving money away did not necessarily lead me to actually doing it.

Most of my life, when they passed the hat around, I wanted to give, but I was afraid if I did, I'd realize soon after that I needed that money for something else. I wanted to give but was afraid I couldn't afford it. I didn't need to judge myself. I needed more information.

I needed to know how much money I actually had, what my expenses actually were, and what the difference actually was between the money I had and the things I needed to pay for. Because in that gap was an amount of money I could afford to give away.

The main thing that budgeting taught me is that, once debts are paid off, there's a lot of room left to help others. It showed me the amount I could afford to give.

After I got a handle on setting an amount each month I was willing to spend on giving, I started challenging myself to pick a number that felt comfortable, and then raised it slightly. This is giving, after all. It's not supposed to be completely comfortable.

But it can be kind of fun.

For example, you know when you're out and unexpectedly someone makes a plug for some charity or cause, and they pass the hat around? People toss in a few dollars if they can. It's actually kind of fun to put forty dollars into the hat. You know that when they go through it later, they'll be really excited by the anonymous donor who really cares about what they're trying to do.

Giving is an opportunity to remind ourselves of what we sense is true, but tend to forget: the point of money is to increase happiness—others' and ours.

IN SEARCH OF OPPORTUNITIES TO GIVE

Research shows millennials are giving back and volunteering their time at a more rapid rate and earlier than previous generations.[101] Pretty great.

Now may not be the ideal time for you to give money away, if you are paying off your student loans. Keep doing that. But if you've wanted to give, and have been frustrated by your own lack of follow-through or confusion about what's the best way to do it, you're not alone.

Let's dive into a few of the specific thoughts that come up when we think about giving our money away.

"I DON'T HAVE MONEY TO GIVE"

This may absolutely be true for you. You don't have it. So here's a thought: if you can't give money away, the best thing you can do is practice socially responsible spending. Don't spend your money on companies whose values you don't support. Take a look at a company's gender diversity policy, racial diversity policy, corporate giving, manufacturing conditions for workers, and corporate tax breaks. Your dollar is your vote, and you can use it to vote for companies who are making the world a better place. Read reviews of companies at www.glassdoor.com and products at www.goodguide.com.

When you don't have money to give, giving time and energy are just as appreciated. As I mentioned, when I was starting out doing comedy, I didn't get paid much—certainly not enough to give it away. Every now and then I would be asked to perform in a benefit comedy show where all the proceeds went to a charity. I was honored to be a part of these events, and they were often my favorites.

I wondered what it would look like to start a comedy charity series, and one time after an open mic, a restaurant owner who had the same thing in mind approached me. Over many meetings and a blossoming friendship and partnership, Comedy for a Cause was born.

Over the next three years, we did over fifty shows, and sold out pretty much every single show. I was able to support comedians by paying a regular wage for their work, and our comedy charity series raised thousands of dollars for all kinds of charities and nonprofits: Make-A-Wish, United Way, Habitat for Humanity, and hurricane rebuilding projects. It didn't cost me any money to make this thing happen, just time and planning that was quickly rewarded through all the great work we got to do and the amazing people we got to meet.

Like my friend, Casey.

Casey and his brother, Colin, have Spinal Muscular Atrophy (SMA). They were age nine and eleven, and were completely incapacitated. They moved around using quadriplegic chairs. I was really honored to raise money for them (we ended up raising over $3,000 to help them by a special van with a lift). I wanted them to feel appreciated, so before the show, I went up to Casey and said, "Hi, Casey. I'm one of the comedians, and I've been really looking forward to meeting you."

Casey looked at me for a second, and then typed into his keyboard, "Make me laugh." I didn't know what to say. Then he hit another button, and a loud man's voice read the sentence. "MAKE ME LAUGH."

So I drew on my years of comedy training, and hundreds of hours writing jokes on every subject there is, and went completely blank. I had nothing.

So I said, "Have a great time Casey. Nice to meet you." Then I sort of slunk back out of the conversation.

That's when I figured out a new slogan for Comedy For A Cause: "Disappointing children since 2011."

"WHERE WOULD I EVEN START?"

When you decide you might like to do something, it's easy to feel overwhelmed at first, because there are so many causes out there. You feel moved to get involved in one, and you're just about to act when you find out about another one, and then another one, and you end up doing nothing. You have cause fatigue, and your inaction doesn't make you feel any better.

Sometimes, when you don't do any research, but rather you simply give money when people ask for it, you can start to feel disconnected and overwhelmed. Instead, focus on giving money to causes you already feel connected to, rather than to whatever cause pops up next.

Sara Montgomery, senior manager of Wells Fargo's philanthropic services department, suggests that a simple cure for this is to "write down three things that are important to you and . . . the last five organizations you've given to."[102] Now, think about whether the two lists have anything in common. If they don't, you can start to do something about that.

"WHAT DIFFERENCE WOULD IT MAKE?"

Comedian Louis C.K. has a painfully honest, thought-provoking joke about choosing inaction over action:

My life is really evil. There are people who are starving in the world, and I drive an Infiniti. That's really evil. There are people who just starve to death. There are people who are born and feel hungry and then die, and that's all they got to do. Meanwhile I'm in my car having a great time, and I sleep like a baby.

It's totally my fault, because I could trade my Infiniti for a really good car. For like a nice Ford Focus with no miles on it, and I'd get back like $20,000. And I could save hundreds of people from dying of starvation with that money, and every single day I don't do it."[103]

That's the kind of fierce and uncomfortable truth Louis C.K. is so skilled at delivering. But he's right that it's easy to feel that if we can't fix the problem then our small contribution doesn't matter. As a result, we get really good at compartmentalizing our compassion, and avoiding thinking about how we can help reduce the suffering of others. The keys here are awareness of, and kindness to, yourself. Now that you notice this, notice how it's influencing your decision to ignore the subject. Remind yourself that you're not responsible for the world's suffering, but you have the opportunity to do something small to make some person's world a little better.

The website of Peter Singer, author of *The Life You Can Save*,[104] breaks down the solution to this tendency by addressing three areas this way: "The tools for personal philanthropy (figuring how much to give and how best to give it), local activism (spreading the word in your community), and political awareness (contacting your representatives to ensure that your nation's foreign aid is really directed to the world's poorest people)."

He offers a list of recommended charities, based on the impact they are having on their area of need: http://www.thelifeyoucansave.org/WheretoDonate.aspx.

Another great resource to measure charities by their impact is The Center for High Impact Philanthropy: http://www.impact.upenn.edu/about/year-end-giving-2013.

So resources like these help us break down the large world of need into some specific places to give, and help your choices make a difference to you.

"HOW DO I KNOW THIS MONEY IS GOING TO THE ACTUAL PEOPLE IN NEED?"

Resources exist, too, that tell you how well the charity of your choice is doing, giving-wise. Give Well supplies a list of "evidence-backed, thoroughly-vetted, underfunded organizations" at www.givewell.org/charities/top-charities. The site discusses each organizations' strengths and weaknesses,[105] as well as explaining how Give Well chooses which charities make it onto the list.[106]

The site Charity Navigator (www.charitynavigator. org) provides info on the operating expenses of charities, including how much they pay their staff and CEOs, and the percent of donations they devote to actual benefits to those in need.

Another way to know where your money actually goes is to check out the website www.givedirectly.org. Rather than offer a way to donate money to a charity, it gives you a way to transfer money directly to people in need. The organization connects the donor with African households, where, according to their website, their average recipient lives on $0.65 per day, and only 15% of households report having enough food in the house for tomorrow.

"I KEEP MEANING TO GIVE, BUT I FORGET."

Totally get it. How many of our intended habits don't ever take off? I would estimate that happens to 100% of the habits we don't make convenient. They're too lofty, they're not actionable, and they're simply not as convenient to make happen as they could be.

Years ago I wanted to really wanted to floss every day.

The way I made it a habit was by making it convenient: I placed floss all over my house. I could never go,

"Oh, it's late and I don't feel like walking to the bathroom to get the floss." I've flossed every day since.

What I discovered was that I was practicing a principle that's been talked about in social psychology.

In his book *The Tipping Point: How Little Things Can Make a Big Difference,* author Malcolm Gladwell relates the findings of social psychologist Howard Levanthal who wanted to see if he could persuade a group of college seniors at Yale University to get a tetanus shot.[107]

Levanthal's research team distributed both "high fear" and "low fear" versions of a pamphlet to students explaining the dangers of tetanus, the importance of inoculation, and letting them know that the shots were free.

The high fear pamphlet had pictures of children having seizures and survivors with tracheotomy wounds and nasal tubes. Yeesh. The low fear pamphlet was kind enough to leave out the photos.

Then they tested which pamphlet achieved greater results. What they found was, as expected, the fear level in the pamphlet definitely affected how freaked out the students were after reading it. But it didn't affect how many of them actually followed up and got their free tetanus shot.

One month after the experiment, only 3% had actually shown up for a shot. It turns out the problem wasn't the level of detail in the pamphlet, but that it had left out two even more important details: the location of the university health building, and the times that shots were available.

What Levanthal discovered was that, as Gladwell writes:

> The students needed to know how to fit the tetanus stuff into their lives; the addition of the map and the times when the shots were available shifted the booklet from an abstract lesson in medical risk—a lesson no different from the countless other academic lessons they had received over their academic career—to a practical and personal piece of medical advice. Once the advice became practical and personal, it became memorable.

So maybe a lot of giving comes down to making it automatic, easy, practical, and convenient. Maybe the best way to start a giving habit is to make it convenient.

There's a website, www.giveback.org, that helps you think through the process of giving through your paycheck. Give Back's mission is a simple yet powerful idea: "To inspire more givers to give more."[108] They describe their process as a way for individuals to start their own foundation, which is pretty cool, but you can also keep it a little less daunting by thinking of it as a way to automatically give a little back whenever you get.

If you use the site, you can review your results at year-end when the Give Back Foundation issues donors a giving statement that can be filed as an IRS tax receipt. There is a one dollar monthly fee for all donation processing, account administration and reward programs. Twelve dollars a year makes giving easy and convenient.

• • • • • • • •

I hope this book has excited you to find ways to give your money, and yourself, to the world around you. It's a pretty rewarding mission statement to give your time, your energy, or your money to those around you who need your help. You'll have a lot of fun along the way, and you'll ensure your perspective on money remains healthy.

If you're lucky, like I was, you'll also meet some children who will truly enjoy the opportunity to laugh in your face. Which might be the best gift of all.

"EPILOGUE"

"Education is the progressive discovery of our own ignorance."

—*Will Durant*

I once learned this Chinese Proverb that said "He who asks a question is a fool for five minutes; he who does not ask a question remains a fool forever."

Mmm. Gooooood proverb! That's not true though, right? Let's be honest, he who asks a question is a fool for as long as he can remember the way people reacted when he asked that question.

When I was in eighth grade, my Spanish teacher was explaining an assignment and referenced Mariah Carey. I wasn't really into music yet (or cool in any way, come to think of it), so I leaned over to my friend and whispered, "Who is Mariah Carey?"

He turned and yelled out, "Colin doesn't know who Mariah Carey is!" Everyone cracked up. My Spanish teacher laughed. My friend laughed. The foreign exchange student from Russia laughed. Even the home-school student who was there for the foreign language credit was laughing.

They laughed and laughed until they couldn't laugh anymore. Then they went on with the lesson, and no one told me who Mariah Carey was.

Pretty funny. But honestly, that moment really stuck with me. Anytime I didn't understand something or wanted to ask a question, I would second-guess myself. I didn't want to sound stupid, and I definitely didn't want to get laughed at by a kid whose principal was also his mom. Believe me, no one got into the Internet faster than me, because suddenly I could Google my stupid questions instead of having to ask them aloud.

Here are some questions the Internet has saved me asking out loud:

"How do I tell if the thing in my kitchen is an oven or a stove?"

"Where do peanuts come from?"

"How many ladybugs does it take to overpower a grown man?"

It's not as many as you think.

Here's the thing: Googling feels safer, but it doesn't really deal with the problem. The real problem is sometimes we don't know something and we have to ask. I figured out how to mask my fear of embarrassment rather than actually get over it. It turned out I was missing an opportunity to grow.

It wasn't until I started learning about personal finance that I was forced to face my lack of understanding. Suddenly I had committed to a job that would entail going into high schools and teaching people about money. I wasn't going to be able to pretend I knew it, and I definitely wasn't going to be able to Google it while onstage. I had to learn it.

I attended workshops on credit, investment, negotiation, and retirement. I read every article I could find, as well as every book I could find, on finance. I asked older people what was working for them. I asked younger people what subject they would actually want to know about.

I asked a lot of questions. And, wouldn't you know it, this simple truth quickly emerged and was reinforced countless times: the quickest way to get the answer is to ask for it.

It's the opposite of the lesson I learned in eighth grade. It's also a way better lesson. Because asking questions might be the single practice that has most affected my own journey to financial knowledge. I stunted my comprehension for years by pretending I understood things I didn't, then I escalated my comprehension every day I chose not to pretend.

I share this story with you because I know how tempting it is when it comes to money to pretend you understand something. Nobody wants to look stupid. Especially when you think you're supposed to already know this by now.

Trust me, there's no reason you're supposed to know this by now. We've already discussed how teachers are not able to cover this subject enough in school, parents are uncomfortable talking about it, and most of the ter- rifyingly-brilliant messaging of consumerism, celebrity, and pop culture deliberately confuses us about how we should think about our money.

The result: too many people don't actually know what they don't actually know. The fact that you are aware of this sets you apart from a lot of people. This awareness is a great thing, because it's the beginning of change.

So be kind to yourself, and practice asking questions. You'll soon see that most people, rather than judge you or think you're stupid, will want to help you understand. But, and this is important: it's up to you to ask.

You can actually have some fun with it. I mean, think about it. It can be kind of funny when you don't know something. It's a classic awkward moment.

Have you ever been in a conversation where someone was explaining something to you, and you did not understand what she or he was talking about? But you didn't want to admit you didn't get it, thinking you might actually be able to smile and nod your way through it?

One time I was talking to this guy at a party, and I asked him what he did for a living. Big mistake. Right away, he lost me. But he thought we were really connecting.

He goes, "Yeah, fourth quarter is really killing us."

So I went, "PFFFT, yeah," while doing kind of a 'totally' gesture. Shrugging while gesturing at nothing. That's it? That was my big move? Yup. Somehow he bought it, so then he KEPT GOING.

"Now we have to sink all this money into this comprehensive P&A strategy."

This time I said, "I mean, you have to."

Again, not a clue what he was talking about. All I can think is, *How did I get myself into this situation? How do I get out of it?* So I asked him where he worked. He gave me the address, and then he started describing the building in ultra-specific detail.

"It's one of these pre-1980, drab, sort-of boxy—anyway, you know what I mean."

No! I really didn't. I didn't know anything about building design. But what I said, in an unexpectedly confident voice, was:

"Well, the 1970s. Not exactly a high water era for architecture."

(To be clear, I also have no idea what that means.)

The guy I was talking to shrugged while gesturing at nothing, and said, "PFFFT, yeah."

I won.

Think about that. I bluffed so convincingly that he didn't understand what I was talking about, while I didn't understand what he was talking about, and we both walked away dumber.

That's pretty stupid, but it is your way out, if you need one. Really lean into it. Just know it's not going to help you understand something new.

When it comes to talking about money, I hope you recognize that moment. Recognize when you want to go "PFFFT yeah." Don't. Fight the temptation. Because the quickest way to get the answer is to ask for it.

So when it comes to personal finance, the best thing you can do is advocate for yourself. Ask questions. Be willing to stop someone and say, "Wait, explain that again. I really need to understand this."

I know at least one person who definitely won't laugh at you. It's the one who wrote this book. Fair enough?

• • • • • • • •

Well, that's it. That's our show.

Writing this book has been a labor of joy, wonder, terror, uncertainty, and love spread over a couple of years and thousands of hours staring at a laptop (in between reading compelling articles like "12 Pictures of Ferrets Holding Golf Clubs"). It's been a difficult task, but it's completely worth it to know you're reading it now.

I called this last part "EPILOGUE" because I've never written a book before and that's what you're supposed call this part. But then I used quotes because, between you and me, it's kind of the wrong word for it. It implies the story is over. But as I told you way back when I shared why I loved the movie *Braveheart* so much: every story starts with a conflict.

A lot of the ideas about money in this book are *guaranteed* to put you in conflict. This book might put you in conflict with your peers, who might think saving money for a dream a long time from now makes you lame. They're wrong. This book might put you in conflict with the messaging of companies that don't particularly want you to be unique, talented, and fulfilled (even though they pretend they do) because they'd rather you were shopping than practicing contentment. They're extra wrong. But most importantly, this book may put you in conflict with yourself, because you've identified money and confidence habits that aren't serving you and need to be changed.

This isn't an epilogue so much as it is the very first page of where your story starts.

You're not going to know it all. But you don't have to. Ask questions. Save money. Build your courage. Be kind. Savor the knowledge that you are writing a story with your life, even in the tough parts. Do your very, very best to have fun with your life. If it helps, know that I'll be out there doing the exact same thing.

ACKNOWLEDGEMENTS

I've been looking forward to saying thank you to the following people for a while now. So here we go:

Thank you to my brilliant reviewing student and educator experts who dissected this book and made it a thousand times better: Zoey, Owen, Sean, Robert, and countless others.

Thank you to Pat, my editor at PGO. Your notes showed me I had something to share, and yours were the powerful extra eyes I needed to whip this book into shape.

Thank you to Angela Palm. Your startling intelligence, insight, and relentless attention to detail helped me construct this into the book I'd hoped it would be. You made me a better writer in the process.

Thank you to the work of brilliant experts James Clear, Jon Acuff, Josh Shipp, and Lindsey Lathrop (to name only a few) who helped me push through the hundreds of hours it took to write this.

Thank you to my friends who functioned as cheerleaders, reminding me to be excited in the often-daunting moments that come while writing a book.

Thank you to my wife, Lindsey, for dreaming with me, laughing with me, and being my best friend.

Most importantly, thank *you* for reading this. It's because of people like you who absorb my work, attend my speeches, and ask fantastically thoughtful questions that I get to say I do this for living.

Your presence always reminds me of the most important lesson: we are not the most important character in our story. Those around us are. When you remember that, you see that your best moments are when you empower, motivate, support, believe in, and listen to those around you. Without them, you would be alone. But with them, you are part of the most important work of all: being human.

ABOUT THE AUTHOR

Colin Ryan is a financial speaker and author with the background of a professional comedian and storyteller.

Colin gives students and adults the money and career skills they'll need to reach their dream. Using humanizing honesty, powerful storytelling, hilarious pop culture touchstones, and a truly inspirational message, Colin helps you transform the dry subject of personal finance into a measurable, actionable, motivating quest for your own fulfillment and freedom. Because your ability to manage your money directly affects your ability to have the life you want.

Colin was named one of the top 10 youth money presenters in America in 2013. To date he has spoken to nearly one million students & adults. He has collaborated with National Geographic Television, the Girl Scouts of America, United Way, and numerous student leadership organizations, as well as banks, credit unions and colleges across the country. He is a Certified Financial Counselor, and his comedy charity series has raised over $150,000 for good causes.

Colin speaks to student and adult audiences nation-wide, and provides financial literacy training for financial institutions, libraries, and schools, and for organization professional development.

Colin won The Moth's storytelling Grand Slam in 2015, and his story, "Saved By The Belle," was featured on National Public Radio, The Moth Radio Hour, and in the Reader's Digest 2016 "Best Stories in America" collection. Most significantly, Colin won his 5th grade regional spelling bee while wearing a Princeton sweater he bought at a thrift store.

ENDNOTES

CHAPTER 1: LET'S TALK ABOUT MONEY

1   Twist, Lynne, and Teresa Barker. *The Soul of Money: Transforming Your Relationship with Money and Life.* New York: Norton, 2003. Print.

2   Mellan, Olivia. *Money Harmony: A Road Map for Individuals and Couples.* S.l.: Money Harmony, 2014. Print.

3   Kilbourne, Jean. *Can't Buy My Love: How Advertising Changes the Way We Think and Feel.* New York: Simon & Schuster, 2000. Print.

CHAPTER 2: CULTURE OF CONSUMPTION

4   "Share of U.S. Workers Living Paycheck to Paycheck Continues Decline from Recession-Era Peak, Finds Annual CareerBuilder Survey." *CareerBuilder.* N.p., 25 Sept. 2013. Web. <http://www.careerbuilder.com/share/aboutus/pressreleasesdetail.aspx?sd=9%2F25%2F2013&id=pr781&ed=12%2F31%2F2013>.

5   "#45 Nicolas Cage - The 2009 Celebrity 100." *Forbes.* Forbes Magazine, 03 June 2009. Web. <http://www.forbes.com/lists/2009/53/celebrity-09_Nicolas-Cage_MCPL.html>.

6   Warner, Brian. "How Did Nicolas Cage Blow Through A $150 Million Dollar Fortune." *Celebrity Net Worth.* N.p., 12 Apr. 2014. Web. <http://www.celebritynetworth.com/articles/celebrity/how-did-nicolas-cage-blow-through-an-150-million-dollar-fortune/>.

7   Bernstein, Jacob. "Nicolas Cage, Compulsive Spender." *The Daily Beast.* Newsweek/Daily Beast, 03 Nov. 2009. Web. <http://www.thedailybeast.com/articles/2009/11/03/nicolas-cage-compulsive-spender.html>.

8   AFP. "Credit-crunched Cage Forced to Sell Castle." *ABC.net.*

Agence France-Presse, 7 Apr. 2009. Web. <http://www.abc.net.au/news/2009-04-08/credit-crunched-cage-forced-to-sell-castle/1644666>.

9   Bera, Sophia. "The Scary State of Financial Literacy in America - DailyFinance." *DailyFinance.com.* AOL Money & Finance, 18 Apr. 2014. Web. <http://www.dailyfinance.com/2014/04/18/the-scary-state-of-financial-literacy-in-america/>.

10   Stanley, Thomas J. *The Millionaire Next Door: The Surprising Secrets of America's Wealthy.* N.p.: Taylor Trade, n.d. *The Millionaire Next Door: Thomas J. Stanley, William D. Danko: 9780671015206: Amazon.com: Books.* 1 Oct. 1998. Web. <http://www.amazon.com/Millionaire-Next-Door-Thomas-Stanley/dp/0671015206>.

11   "Payroll Tax News at National Payroll Week.com." *Getting Paid in America 2014 Survey.* National Payroll Week.com, 2014. Web. <http://www.nationalpayrollweek.com/news.cfm>.

12   FINRA Investor Education Foundation. *FINRA Foundation Releases Nation's First State-by-State Financial Capability Survey.* FINRA Foundation, 8 Dec. 2010. Web. <http://www.usfinancialcapability.org/pr_12082010.html>.

13   Kaplan, Michael. "6 Ways Las Vegas Security Tech Has Entered Daily Life." *Popular Mechanics.* N.p., 1 Jan. 2010. Web. <http://www.popularmechanics.com/technology/how-to/computer-security/4341500>.

14   Chatzky, Jean. *Money Rules: The Simple Path to Lifelong Security.* N.p.: Rodale, 2012. Print.

15   Tufts, Andrew. "One Click Root." *One Click Root.* N.p., 05 Mar. 2014. Web. <https://www.oneclickroot.com/android-manufacturers/how-much-did-samsung-pay-for-ellens-oscars-selfie/>.

16   *The Story of Stuff.* Perf. Annie Leonard. Free Range Studios, 2007. <https://www.youtube.com/watch?v=9GorqroigqM.>

17   Rainie, Harrison, and Barry Wellman. *Networked: The New Social Operating System.* Cambridge, MA: MIT, 2012. Print.

18   Troianovski, Anton. "Cellphones Are Eating the Family Budget." *The Wall Street Journal.* Dow Jones & Company, 28 Sept. 2012. Web. <http://online.wsj.com/news/articles/SB10000872396390444083304578018731890309450>.

19   Troianovski, Anton. "Cellphones Are Eating the Family Budget." *The Wall Street Journal*. Dow Jones & Company, 28 Sept. 2012. Web. <http://online.wsj.com/news/articles/SB10000872 3963904440833045780187318903090450>.

20   *Roger Dodger*. Dir. Dylan Kidd. Perf. Campbell Scott, Jesse Eisenberg, Isabella Rossellini. Holedigger Films, 2002. DVD. <http://www.imdb.com/title/tt0299117/>

21   *IMDb*. IMDb.com, n.d. Web. 04 Jan. 2016. <http://www.imdb. com/title/tt0804503/>.

22   Noble, Oliver. "A Brief History of Conspicuous Product Placement in Movies." *YouTube*. Filmdrunk.Uproxx, 9 Jan. 2011. Web. <https://www.youtube.com/watch?v=wACBAu9coUU>.

23   *Casino Royale (2006)*. Dir. Martin Campbell. Perf. Daniel Craig, Eva Green, Judi Dench. MGM, 2006. DVD. <http://www. imdb.com/title/tt0381061/>

24   "Christmas Conspiracy." *Vimeo*. NGEN Radio, n.d. Web. 21 Nov. 2014. <http://vimeo.com/32601878>.

25   "Consumer Reports Poll: Consumers Plan To Cut Back On Holiday Spending Less So Than In 'Recession' Years: Consumer Reports Http://pressroom.consumerreports.org/pressroom/." *Consumer Reports 2014*. N.p., 28 Oct. 2010. Web. <http:// pressroom.consumerreports.org/pressroom/2010/10/consumer-reports-poll-consumers-plan-to-cut-back-on-holiday-spending-less-so-than-in-recession-years-1.html>.

26   "2014 Planned Christmas Spending." *2014 Planned Christmas Spending*. American Research Group, Inc., 21 Nov. 2014. Web. <http://www.americanresearchgroup.com/holiday/>.

27   McMillan, Rob. "Black Friday Frenzy: Beaumont Friends Camp out 3 Weeks Early." *ABC7 Los Angeles*. N.p., 11 Nov. 2014. Web. <http://abc7.com/shopping/black-friday-frenzy-beaumont-friends-camp-out-3-weeks-early/391115/>.

28   Stewart, James. "Black Friday Campouts: As Traditional as Turkey." *The New York Times*. The New York Times, 21 Nov. 2014. Web. <http://www.nytimes.com/2014/11/22/business/black-friday-campouts-as-traditional-as-turkey.html?_r=0>.

29   Levin, Ryan. "The Critique of Consumerism in George Romero's 'Dawn of the Dead' (1978)." *The Man in the Movie Hat*.

N.p., n.d. Web. 21 Nov. 2014. <http://www.themaninthemoviehat.com/what-you-should-be-watching-george-romeros-dawn-of-the-dead-1978/>.

30   "United States Personal Savings Rate 1959-2014 | Data | Chart | Calendar." *United States Personal Savings Rate.* Ed. Anna Fedec. Trading Economics, n.d. Web. 06 Oct. 2014. <http://www.tradingeconomics.com/united-states/personal-savings>.

31   "Household Net Saving Rates." *OECD Factbook 2014: Economic, Environmental and Social Statistics.* OECD Publishing, 6 May 2014. Web. <http://www.oecd-ilibrary.org/economics/oecd-factbook_18147364>. *A note: the household saving rate is calculated as the ratio of household savings to household disposable income (plus the change in net equity of households in pension funds). Household savings are estimated by subtracting household expenditures from household disposable income, plus the change in net equity of households in pension funds. Minus sign (–) indicates an excess of expenditures over income]*

32   "Economics: Key Tables from OECD." *OECD Factbook 2014: Economic, Environmental and Social Statistics.* OECD Publishing, 6 May 2014. Web. <http://www.oecd-ilibrary.org/economics/household-saving-rates-forecasts_2074384x-table7>.

33   Garon, Sheldon M. *Beyond Our Means: Why America Spends While the World Saves.* Princeton, NJ: Princeton UP, 2012. Print.

CHAPTER 3: BUYING TIME

34   Bissonnette, Zac. *How to Be Richer, Smarter, and Better-looking than Your Parents.* New York: Portfolio/Penguin, 2012. Print.

35   Lehrer, Jonah. "Don't! - The New Yorker." *The New Yorker.* N.p., 18 May 2009. Web. <http://www.newyorker.com/magazine/2009/05/18/dont-2>.

36   Tierney, John. "Do You Suffer From Decision Fatigue?" *New York Times.* N.p., 17 Aug. 2011. Web. <http://www.nytimes.com/2011/08/21/magazine/do-you-suffer-from-decision-fatigue.html>.

37   Spiegel, Alix. "Is Your Personality Fixed, Or Can You Change Who You Are?" Audio podcast. Invisibilia. June 24, 2016. Web.

38   Renzulli, Kerri Anne. "Why the $245,000 Cost of Raising a

Child Shouldn't Stop You From Having One." *Money.* Time, Inc., 8 Apr. 2014. Web. <http://time.com/money/3136260/245340-usda-cost-of-raising-a-child-having-baby-245000-304480-department-of-agriculture/>.

39   Bernardo, Richie. "The True Cost of Smoking by State." *WalletHub.* N.p., n.d. Web. <https://wallethub.com/edu/the-financial-cost-of-smoking-by-state/9520/#cost-lifetime>.

40   *Since tracking millennials for their entire working lives would require time travel, the most recent reference point for this comes from the Bureau of Labor Statistics National Longitudinal Survey of Youth 1979 (NLSY79), which tracked younger baby boomers from ages 18 to 46: On average, men held 11.4 jobs and women held 10.7 jobs. 26% held 15 jobs or more, while 10% held zero to four jobs.* "Number of Jobs Held, Labor Market Activity, and Earnings Growth among the Youngest Baby Boomers: Results from a Longitudinal Survey." *Number of Jobs Held, Labor Market Activity, and Earnings Growth among the Youngest Baby Boomers: Results from a Longitudinal Survey* (n.d.): n. pag. 25 July 2012. Web. <http://www.bls.gov/news.release/pdf/nlsoy.pdf>. Note: *One drawback to this study is that it does not reflect the labor market behavior of people who are older or younger than the baby boomers in the survey or who immigrated to the United States after the survey began in 1979.)*

41   *The Lookout.* Dir. Scott Frank. By Scott Frank. Prod. Roger Birnbaum and Gary Barber. Perf. Joseph Gordon-Levitt, Jeff Daniels, and Matthew Goode. Miramax Films, 2007. DVD.

42   "One in Three Americans Prepare a Detailed Household Budget." *Gallup.* Gallup Poll, 4 April 2013. Web. <http://www.gallup.com/poll/162872/one-three-americans-prepare-detailed-household-budget.aspx>.

43   Chatzky, Jean. *Money Rules: The Simple Path to Lifelong Security.* N.p.: Rodale, 2012. Print.

CHAPTER 4: DEFEATING DEBT

44   Friedline, Terri, and Stacia West. *Financial Education Is Not Enough: Millennials May Need Financial Capability for Healthy Financial Behaviors.* The University of Kansas, 01 May 2015.

Web. <https://aedi.ku.edu/sites/aedi.ku.edu/files/docs/publication/Working-Papers/WP02-15.pdf>.

45 Benett, Andrew, and Ann O'Reilly. "The End of Hyperconsumerism." *The Atlantic*. Atlantic Media Company, 28 July 2010. Web. <http://www.theatlantic.com/business/archive/2010/07/the-end-of-hyperconsumerism/60558/>.

46 *Confessions of a Shopaholic*. Dir. P. J. Hogan. Prod. Jerry Bruckheimer. By Tracey Jackson, Tim Firth, and Kayla Alpert. Perf. Isla Fisher, Hugh Dancy, and Joan Cusack. Walt Disney Studios Motion Pictures, 2009. DVD.

47 Jendrysik, Ted. ""Perfect Life"" *YouTube*. YouTube, 20 May 2011. Web. <https://www.youtube.com/watch?v=PV_YAe-XOSiw>.

48 Prelec, Drazen, and Duncan Simester. "Always Leave Home without It: A Further Investigation of the Credit-Card Effect on Willingness to Pay." *Marketing Letters* 12.1 (2001): 5-12. JSTOR. Web. <http://www.jstor.org/stable/10.2307/40216581?ref=-search-gateway:f9ded958449e58f858858c361f642884>.

49 Konsko, Lindsay. "Credit Cards Make You Spend More: Studies - NerdWallet." *NerdWallet*. NerdWallet, 08 July 2014. Web. <https://www.nerdwallet.com/blog/credit-cards/credit-cards-make-you-spend-more/>.

50 *New Car. New Car*. Free Credit Report, 2007. Web. 1 May 2016. <https://www.youtube.com/watch?v=wzPkhOofXVs>.

51 "Deadbeat." *Credit Card Glossary: Terms and Definitions*. CreditCards.com, n.d. Web. 31 Oct. 2014. <http://www.creditcards.com/glossary/term-deadbeat.php>.

52 Gerson, Emily S., and Ben Woolsey. "The History of Credit Cards." *CreditCards.com News*. N.p., 11 May 2009. Web. <http://www.creditcards.com/credit-card-news/credit-cards-history-1264.php>.

53 "Deregulation." *What-When-How*. N.p., n.d. Web. 31 Oct. 2014. <http://what-when-how.com/the-american-economy/deregulation/>.

54 Beck, Jackie. "Debt Is Not Forever." *The Debt Myth*. N.p., 29 Dec. 2014. Web. <http://www.thedebtmyth.com/debt-is-not-forever>.

CHAPTER 5: MAKING MONEY

55   Cuban, Mark. "Don't Follow Your Passion, Follow Your Effort." *Blog Maverick - The Mark Cuban Weblog.* N.p., 8 Mar. 2012. Web.   <http://blogmaverick.com/2012/03/18/dont-follow-your-passion-follow-your-effort/>.

56   *Outliers: The Story of Success.* Reprint ed. N.p.: Back Bay, 2011. Print.

57   *The Denver Post: Business.* Digital First Media, 15 Nov. 2014. Web. <http://www.nationalskillscoalition.org/news/latest/business-must-take-lead-in-filling-thousands-of-middle-skill-jobs>.

58   Wright, Joshua. "The Associate's Degree Payoff: Community College Grads Can Get High-Paying Jobs, and Here Are Some Examples." *EMSI Economic Modeling Specialists Intl.* N.p., 06 May 2013. Web. <http://www.economicmodeling.com/2013/05/06/the-associates-degree-payoff-community-college-grads-can-get-high-paying-jobs-and-here-are-some-examples/>.

59   Vestic, Ben. "Small Business Failure Rate - 9 Out of 10?" *Ezine Articles.* N.p., 24 Sept. 2010. Web. <http://ezinearticles.com/?Small-Business-Failure-Rate---9-Out-of-10?&id=5089437>.

60   Luscombe, Belinda. "Do We Need $75,000 a Year to Be Happy?" *Time.* Time Inc., 06 Sept. 2010. Web. <http://content.time.com/time/magazine/article/0,9171,2019628,00.html>.

61   "2011 Teens & Money Survey." *Schwab MoneyWise.* Charles Schwab, 2011. Web. <http://www.schwabmoneywise.com/public/moneywise/calculators_tools/families_money_surveys/teens_money_survey>.

62   "Current Population Survey, 2011 Annual Social and Economic Supplement." *United States Census Bureau.* N.p., 2011. Web. <http://www.census.gov/hhes/www/cpstables/032011/perinc/new01_001.htm>.

63   Stanley, Thomas J. *The Millionaire Next Door: The Surprising Secrets of America's Wealthy.* N.p.: Taylor Trade, n.d. *The Millionaire Next Door: Thomas J. Stanley, William D. Danko: 9780671015206: Amazon.com: Books.* 1 Oct. 1998. Web. <http://www.amazon.com/Millionaire-Next-Door-Thomas-Stanley/dp/0671015206>.

64   "The Life of a Bond." *BlackRock Blog Global Market Intelli-*

gence. N.p., 22 Apr. 2014. Web. <http://www.blackrockblog. com/2014/04/22/lifecycle/>. *If you prefer this visually, this is a helpful infographic.*

65   Financial Literacy in College | Financial Literacy Video. *You-Tube.* IGrad, 16 Dec. 2011. Web. <https://www.youtube.com/ watch?v=I_ZbOPnL7_M>.

66   "Historical Inflation Rates: 1914-2014." *US Inflation Calculator.* N.p., n.d. Web. 03 Oct. 2014. <http://www.usinflationcalculator.com/inflation/historical-inflation-rates/>.

67   Lazeba, Alexander. "Investing Money in Plain English." *You-Tube.* CommonCraft, 29 Jan. 2013. Web. <http://www.youtube.com/watch?v=2YhfDruQnqs>.

68   "Day Trading: Your Dollars at Risk." *SEC.gov.* N.p., n.d. Web. 21 Nov. 2014. <http://www.sec.gov/investor/pubs/daytips. htm>.

69   Haisley, Emily; Mostafa, Romel; Loewenstein, George. "Myopic Risk-seeking: The Impact of Narrow Decision Bracketing on Lottery Play - Springer." *Journal of Risk and Uncertainty 37.1 (2008): 57-75. Springer Link.* Springer US, 01 Aug. 2008. Web. <http://link.springer.com/article/10.1007/s11166-008-9041-1>.

70   "Lottery Winner Statistics." *Statistic Brain.* Camelot Group PLC, 26 July 2014. Web. <http://www.statisticbrain.com/lottery-winner-statistics/>.

71   Chang, David. "Financial Lessons From Broke Lottery Winners." *The Art of Thinking Smart.* N.p., 3 July 2013. Web. <http://artofthinkingsmart.com/lessons-from-lottery-winners/>.

72   "What Could Happen to You: Tales of Big Lottery Winners." *NBC News.* N.p., 17 May 2013. Web. <http://usnews. nbcnews.com/_news/2013/05/17/18323470-what-could-happen-to-you-tales-of-big-lottery-winners>.

73   Williams, Geoff. "Poor People Spend 9% of Income on Lottery Tickets; Here's Why - DailyFinance." *DailyFinance.com.* N.p., 31 May 2010. Web. <http://www.dailyfinance.com/2010/05/31/ poor-people-spend-9-of-income-on-lottery-tickets-heres-why/>.

74   Wolff, Richard D. "Lotteries as Disguised, Regressive, and

Counterproductive Taxes." *Professor Richard D. Wolff.* N.p., 9 Mar. 2011. Web. <http://rdwolff.com/content/lotteries-disguised-regressive-and-counterproductive-taxes>.

75   Haisley, Emily; Mostafa, Romel; Loewenstein, George. "Myopic Risk-seeking: The Impact of Narrow Decision Bracketing on Lottery Play - Springer." *Journal of Risk and Uncertainty 37.1 (2008): 57-75. Springer Link.* Springer US, 01 Aug. 2008. Web. <http://link.springer.com/article/10.1007/s11166-008-9041-1>.

76   *Live Free or Die Hard.* Dir. Len Wiseman. Prod. Michael Fottrell. By Mark Bomback and David Marconi. Perf. Bruce Willis, Justin Long, and Timothy Olyphant. Twentieth Century-Fox Film Corp., 2007. DVD.

77   Appleby, Denise. "Roth Vs. Traditional IRA: Which Is Right For You?" *Investopedia.* N.p., n.d. Web. 21 Nov. 2014. <http://www.investopedia.com/articles/retirement/03/012203.asp#axzz2B-SyCpEQb>.

QUICK GUIDE: HIGHER EDUCATION

78   *Forbes.* Forbes Magazine, 1 Sept. 2015. Web. <http://www.forbes.com/sites/nicholaswyman/2015/09/01/why-we-desperately-need-to-bring-back-vocational-training-in-schools/>.

79   "Types of Colleges: The Basics." *Types of Colleges: The Basics.* N.p., n.d. Web. <https://bigfuture.collegeboard.org/find-colleges/college-101/types-of-colleges-the-basics>.

80   "Credit Card Statistics." *College Student Credit Card.* N.p., n.d. Web. 22 Dec. 2014. <http://collegestudentcreditcard.com/articles11.html>.

81   Barr, Cecilia. "Student Loan Debt: Statistics, Solutions & Crisis Help." *Student Loan Debt Statistics.* Debt.org, n.d. Web. <https://www.debt.org/students/debt/>.

82   Ghahremani, Yasmin, and Tamara Holmes. "Credit Card Debt Statistics." *CreditCards.com News.* N.p., 23 Sept. 2014. Web. <http://www.creditcards.com/credit-card-news/credit-card-debt-statistics-1276.php>.

83   Williams, Fred O. "Average American Expects to Be Debt Free by Age 53." *CreditCards.com News.* N.p., 23 July 2013. Web.

<http://www.creditcards.com/credit-card-news/debt-free-age-53-1276.php>.

84 Crouch, Michelle. "Poll: Card Debt the No. 1 Taboo Subject." *CreditCards.com News*. N.p., 15 Apr. 2013. Web. <http://www.creditcards.com/credit-card-news/poll-credit-card-taboo-subject-2013-1276.php>.

85 Harrington, Rebecca. "College Graduates Earn 84% More Than High School Grads, Study Says." The Huffington Post. TheHuffingtonPost.com, 05 Aug. 2011. Web. 31 July 2013. <http://www.huffingtonpost.com/2011/08/05/college-graduates-earn-84_n_919579.html>.

86 "College Savings Plan Network 2012." *CollegeSavings.org*. College Savings Plan Network, Sept. 2012. Web. 31 July 2013. <http://www.collegesavings.org/includes/pdfs/Sept%202012%20529%20Report.pdf>.

87 The College Board. "Individual and Societal Benefits of Higher Education." Education Pays 2010 2010: 10. Web. 31 July 2013. <http://trends.collegeboard.org/sites/default/files/education-pays-2010-full-report.pdf>.

88 "The Occupational Outlook." *Good.is*. Good Worldwide Inc, 2013. Web. <http://magazine.good.is/infographics/interactive-infographic-the-occupational-outlook>.

89 Rose, Cecilia, and Lisa Barrow. "Does College Still Pay?" *The Economist's Voice* 2.4 (2005): n. pag. Web. 14 Jan. 2015. <http://www.econ.ku.dk/okojacob/MAKRO-E05/article-education.pdf>.

90 Wadsworth, Gordon H. "Sky Rocketing College Costs." InflationData.com. N.p., 14 June 2013. Web. 31 July 2013. <http://inflationdata.com/Inflation/Inflation_Articles/Education_Inflation.asp>.

91 Kingkade, Tyler. "Student Loan Debt: New Reports Find 'Unsustainable' Trend Dragging Economy." The Huffington Post. TheHuffingtonPost.com, 31 Jan. 2013. Web. 31 July 2013. <http://www.huffingtonpost.com/2013/01/31/student-loan-debt-unsustainable_n_2593303.html>.

92 Nance-Nash, Sheryl. "Student Loan Debt: $1 Trillion and Counting." Forbes. Forbes Magazine, 22 Mar. 2012. Web.

31 July 2013. <http://www.forbes.com/sites/sherylnance-nash/2012/03/22/student-loan-debt-1-trillion-and-counting/>.

93 Edwards, Greg. "Fed: Student Loan Debt Surpasses Auto, Credit Card Debt." St. Louis Business Journal. St. Louis Business Journal, 24 Apr. 2013. Web. 31 July 2013. <http://www.bizjournals.com/stlouis/blog/2013/04/fed-student-loan-debt-surpasses-auto.html>.

94 *Accepted.* Dir. Steve Pink. Perf. Justin Long, Jonah Hill, Blake Lively. Universal Pictures, Shady Acres Entertainment, 2006. DVD.

95 Baum, Sandy, Jennifer Ma, and Kathleen Payea. "Education Pays 2013 - The Benefits of Higher Education for Individuals and Society." *Trends in Higher Education Series.* CollegeBoard, 2013. Web. <http://trends.collegeboard.org/education-pays>.

96 "One-Third of College-Educated Workers Do Not Work in Occupations Related to Their College Major." *CareerBuilder.* N.p., 11 Nov. 2014. Web. <http://www.careerbuilder.com/share/aboutus/pressreleasesdetail.aspx?sd=11%2f14%2f2013&siteid=cb-pr&sc_cmp1=cb_pr790_&id=pr790&ed=12%2f31%2f2013>.

97 Chatzky, Jean. *Money Rules: The Simple Path to Lifelong Security.* N.p.: Rodale, 2012. Print.

98 "Student Loan Debt Statistics." *Student Loan Hero.* N.p., n.d. Web. 3 Oct. 2016. <https://studentloanhero.com/student-loan-debt-statistics/>.

99 *Quick Facts about Student Debt.* Rep. National Center for Education Statistics - The Institute for College Access & Success, 1 Mar. 2014. Web. <http://projectonstudentdebt.org/files/pub/Debt_Facts_and_Sources.pdf>.

QUICK GUIDE: MINI-PHILANTHROPY

100 Hill, Libby. "After 500th Make-A-Wish Request, WWE Superstar John Cena Says He'd 'Drop Everything' to Do It Again." *Los Angeles Times.* Los Angeles Times, 21 Aug. 2015. Web. <http://www.latimes.com/entertainment/tv/showtracker/la-et-st-john-cena-grants-500th-wish-20150821-htmlstory.html>.

101 Goldberg, Eleanor. "Millennials Are Volunteering More Than Past Generations And Haven't Even Peaked Yet." *The Huffington*

Post. TheHuffingtonPost.com, 4 Dec. 2015. Web. <http://www.huffingtonpost.com/entry/millennials-are-eager-to-donate-their-biggest-asset-time_us_5661a464e4b072e9d1c5b68a>.

102   Sharf, Samantha. "How To Give Away Money When It Feels Like You Don't Have Any." *Forbes.* Forbes Magazine, 11 Dec. 2013. Web. <http://www.forbes.com/sites/samantha-sharf/2013/12/11/how-to-give-away-money-when-it-feels-like-you-dont-have-any/>.

103   *Louie, Season 3 Episode 1: Something Is Wrong.* Dir. Louis CK. Perf. Louis CK. 3 Arts Entertainment, Bluebush Productions, FX Productions. 2012. TV.

104   Singer, Peter. "The Life You Can Save: How to Do Your Part to End World Poverty." *The Life You Can Save: How to Do Your Part to End World Poverty.* Random House, 14 Sept. 2010. Web.   <http://www.amazon.com/The-Life-You-Can-Save/dp/0812981561>.

105   Karnofsky, Holden. "GiveWell's Top Charities for Giving Season 2013." *The GiveWell Blog.* The Clear Fund, 1 Dec. 2013. Web. <http://blog.givewell.org/2013/12/01/givewells-top-charities-for-giving-season-2013/>.

106   "GiveWell: Process for Identifying Top Charities." *GiveWell.* N.p., Nov. 2013. Web. <http://www.givewell.org/international/process>.

107   Gladwell, Malcolm. *The Tipping Point: How Little Things Can Make a Big Difference.* Boston: Little, Brown, 2000. Print.

108   *GiveBack.* N.p., 2010. Web. <http://www.giveback.org/>.

CPSIA information can be obtained
at www.ICGtesting.com
Printed in the USA
LVW021151260321